Mother, Should I Trust the Government?

Watch a presentation by Jake Jacobs, Ph.D.

Mother, Should I Trust the Government?

The Making and Keeping of our American Republic

Jake Jacobs, Ph.D.

LIFE SENTENCE
Publishing, LLC

Visit Jake's website: www.jjusa.org

Mother, Should I Trust the Government? – Jake Jacobs, Ph.D.

Copyright © 2014

First edition published 2014

Cover Design: Amber Burger

Cover Image, Coin: Lane V. Erickson/Shutterstock

Editors: Mary Vesperman, Sheila Wilkinson

Cartoons: A.F. Branco, used by permission

Printed in the United States of America

www.lifesentencepublishing.com

LIFE SENTENCE Publishing books are available at discounted prices for ministries and other outreach.
Find out more by contacting us at info@lspbooks.com

LIFE SENTENCE Publishing, and its logo are trademarks of

LIFE SENTENCE Publishing, LLC
P.O. Box 652
Abbotsford, WI 54405

POLITICAL SCIENCE / History & Theory

Paperback ISBN: 978-1-62245-231-6

Ebook ISBN: 978-1-62245-232-3

10 9 8 7 6 5 4 3 2 1

This book is available from www.amazon.com, Barnes & Noble, and your local bookstore.

Share this book on Facebook:

Contents

This book is dedicated to my Mother, Jessie Jacobs, who dedicated her life to taking care of her family. Thanks Mom for loving us so well!

It is also dedicated to America's Founding Mothers who from Abigail Adams to Martha Washington were willing to give of their lives, fortunes, sacred honor, and husbands for Liberty in America.

And it is dedicated to my children's mother, my lovely wife Lori, whose dedication to our family helped make our kids so very special.

I want to thank Anthony Branco for the use of his brilliant political cartoons throughout my book. Please visit his website COMICALLY INCORRECT CARTOONS by A.F. Branco and enjoy his talent on loan from God: http://comicallyincorrect.com/

INTRODUCTION

*Wherever the real power in a Government lies, there
is the danger of oppression.*
—James Madison

A s I am writing my new book, *Mother Should I Trust the
Government?*, during the summer of AD 2014, the news
has been inundated with stories upon stories about Federal government scandals, cover-ups, deception, hypocrisy, duplicity,
and just plain old-fashioned government corruption. From the
VA, DOJ, IRS, and NSA to the EPA, DOE, and DOT, we find
the concerns of our Founding Fathers like Thomas Jefferson,
Patrick Henry, George Mason, Samuel Adams, and many others
about the inevitable corruption of a Central-National-Federal
government have prophetically come to fruition. When President
Barack Obama was asked about the IRS's scandalous scrutinizing of Tea Party organizations, he arrogantly dismissed the
charges by saying there's "not even a smidgen of corruption." A
few days later the head of the Federal government's Progressive
Internal Revenue Service told a Senate investigative committee that they lost the e-mail hard drive that would reveal the
details of much more than a smidgen of evidence that would

indict the taxmen of America! Something "stinketh" not only in Denmark but in Washington, D.C., and it's not the Potomac River; it's the smell of government lies that have plagued mankind from time immemorial.

This little book is designed to be a simple explanation of our Founders' vision of a republican form of government where the people and the States were to be sovereign, while stressing that the Federal government was to have only a few, very few, limited and explicitly listed enumerated powers given to them by the people. It will also be an exposé of stories where the Federal and at times State governments have abused their designated powers and violated the God-given sovereignty of life and liberty for American citizens.

Why the title *Mother, Should I Trust the Government?* I remember as a kid in the 1960s and 1970s asking my mother all kinds of questions about life, love, God, sex, music, movies, World War II, and the government. The Sixties, you will recall, was a turbulent time in the world of government, as there were Vietnam War protests, civil rights demonstrations, and socialist and communist radicals like Barack Obama's buddies Bill Ayers and Bernadine Dohrn calling for revolution in the streets as they bombed various government facilities. My mother and I had many great discussions on sundry issues, as we still do today.

While she is my biggest advocate, she will also once in a while give me gentle advice or critique my work. She did not like the title of my last book, *MOBOCRACY,* or that it was in hard cover. She asked that I show her the rough draft cover of the book you are presently reading. My lovely mother is eighty-nine years old and unfortunately not in the best of health. She has very bad vision and lives in a nursing home.

I made a copy of the book cover with the title and printed it in big letters, put it in a stand-up, plastic holder, and placed it on a table next to her chair without telling her it was the book cover. She looked at the cover title *Mother, Should I Trust the Government?* And, thinking I was asking her a question, she simply looked at me and said, "**** No!" When I told her it was the rough-draft cover of my new book, we both laughed so hard it hurt. Whether it is our Founding Fathers or my lovely mother, the bottom line response is almost always: "**** No!"

Notice I said "almost always," not always. It must be stressed over and over again that our Founding Fathers were NOT anarchists who advocated no government in America. While anarchists may rightfully have a profound distrust of all government, their utopic vision of a world without government is not only naïve and sophomoric, it does not deal with the reality of the government being needed in society to prevent chaos and mob rule.

Some form of "government" has been a part of man's existence since the beginning of time. The all-time, zillion-dollar question for those who cherish life and liberty is:

How much government is necessary to preserve life and liberty?

Political philosophers, historians, tyrants, despots, statesmen, and politicians have articulated and debated various forms of government throughout history, usually leaving out the self-evident truth that all men are created equal by God and given the precious gifts of life and liberty, free from government control. The genius of our Founders is that after centuries of searching for the answer to the government question, their answer was our wonderful **Republic under God!**

Historically anarchists were cousins to communists and shared many of the same ideas that rejected and repudiated our Founders' **republican, limited government** world-view. They parted with the Marxist dialectic known as the "dictatorship of the proletariat" where the socialistic State would destroy republicanism, private property, free enterprise as a social and economic system, and religion as revealed in Judaism and Christianity. Anarchists also rejected the absolute, idiotic, Marxist concept that the State would magically "wither away" someday, thus creating a pure, lovely, peaceful, communistic, one-world, government-less society. Anarchy's idiocy of "no government ever" could never join with Karl Marx's idiocy of an all-powerful, totalitarian State withering away.

Our Founding Fathers did not deal with godless, man-centered, pie-in-the-sky, utopic theories that had no anchoring in the real world of sinful fallen man, who was also fearfully and wonderfully made in the image of God. Our Founders not only studied Greek philosophy in Greek and Roman republicanism in Latin, but many of them studied government and the human condition in Hebrew and Greek as understood in the *Torah-Tanach* and *Brit Chadashah,* or what we call the Old and New Testaments. Unlike Enlightenment, French revolutionary, communist, and anarchist thinkers, our Founders' political worldview was not only influenced by the Greco-Roman world, it was profoundly shaped by the Judeo-Christian and Anglo-Saxon world that was solidly imbedded within a biblical paradigm. This classic Christian Western civilization education was taught at Christian universities, such as Cambridge, Oxford, Paris, and Padua, and then transplanted by our forefathers to Harvard, Yale, William and Mary, Brown, and Princeton, creating an understanding of man that clearly understood that "if men were angels there'd be no need for government." Unlike anarchists, America's Founders realistically concluded that since men were not angels, government comprised of men must be: **LIMITED, checked, balanced, separated, republican, and watched like a hawk forever!**

Our Founders understood that since government was made up of flawed, sinful human beings, with the potential to be just and lawful, it was imperative to reinforce a moral persuasion upon the character of government leaders to reinforce the temperament of limited, balanced government.

Their constitutional formula was a delicate balance of enough State power to protect the citizen's unalienable, God-given life and liberty, while not allowing too much State power to harm the citizen.

As students of history, our Founders saw that most

government or State rulers such as Kings, Queens, Lords, Nobles, et.al, were usually not looking out for the best interests of their subjects and subjected them to abuse in perpetual servitude and serfdom. A couple classic examples of this occur in the stories of the Scotsman William Wallace as depicted in the famed 1995 Oscar- winning film *Braveheart* and the classic tale of the Englishman *Robin Hood* of Sherwood Forest.

In *Braveheart* the main character, William Wallace, represents the people of Scotland who have been oppressed by the English monarchy for centuries. As a young lad, Wallace knows that the King of England, Edward I, has murdered clan Chieftains and his family, and upon returning home after many years away, all he wants to do is live his life in liberty in his **"thatched roof castle,"** free from government control. Despising and defying the King's decree of sharing one's wife with the King and his Nobles, Wallace has a Christian marriage in secret. When the soldiers of the King's occupying government attempt to rape Wallace's wife, he defends his family. One of the King's Nobles executes her as revenge. The rest of the story is the age-old battle of an oppressed people crying out "give me liberty or give me death!" And understanding that Liberty to them was freedom from government oppression, many Scotsmen did die, while all along simply wanting to be left alone in their **thatched roof castles.**

This concept of a free citizen's **thatched roof castle** was: **The fundamental idea of Life and Liberty** that developed in Western Christian civilization led up to the 1776

Declaration of Independence versus, once again, a tyrannical king of England. The Founding Father James Otis, the brilliant lawyer, orator, and member of the Massachusetts Assembly, stressed over and over again in his legal argumentation against the King of England:

> "One of the most essential branches of English liberty is the freedom of one's house. A man's house is his castle."

This work is not an indictment of all of England's rulers, way of life, or of all government at all times. Many of our Founders' ideas came from English and Scottish political theory, and there were great Christian kings like Canute the Great and Alfred the Great who helped establish God's law as the foundation of English Common Law, which developed into Parliamentary Law, which in turn influenced our **republican form of government**. I love England and I love our "English republican" roots. I travel there all the time to see my many dear English friends; I have taught there, went to the University of Brighton for a semester, and received my Ph.D. in London. However, like our Founders, it is English tyranny I despise, as I do when our government is tyrannical.

Another example of **thatched roof castle** oppression is in the classic English story of *Robin Hood*. We are told over and over again by liberal pundits who love the class warfare argument on the rich in America that Robin Hood stole from the rich and gave to the poor, thus justifying the Federal government's progressive, punitive "the more you make, the more we take" taxation. They conveniently leave out the most important component of the story.

Robin Hood took the people's stolen property back from an oppressive criminal government and gave it to the people who produced and owned the property in the first place.

Robin Hood believed in the rule of law and served the honorable King Richard the Lionhearted, but it was when Richard's brother, the tyrannical King John I of Magna Charta fame, violated the rule of law, that Robin Hood and his band of merry freedom fighters gave back to the people living in their **thatched roof castles** the property confiscated by their government.

Real-life stories or tales like *Braveheart* and *Robin Hood* reflect the centuries-old battle between what became known by English and Scottish political philosophers as *REX LEX* versus *LEX REX*. *REX LEX* was the arrogant worldview held by monarchs that the king was not only THE Law, but he was above the Law or a Law unto himself. Thus what he declared, whether it aligned with the Sovereign King of the Universe's Law or not, was irrelevant. Gradually as Liberty fighters and philosophers fought this evil anti-Christian idea, there evolved the foundations of our Declaration of Independence and our constitutional republican form of government the wonderful idea of *LEX REX,* or Law is King or Law is above the King. Ultimately that Law was God's Law.

This concept was in relationship to the development of what became known as "The Doctrine of the Lesser

Magistrates," where government officials under the king believed that if the king violated the Law of the Supreme Judge of the World, our Creator, then it was proper to resist tyranny and not to blindly follow and obey evil civil government. In early 1776 Thomas Paine published a patriotic pamphlet titled *Common Sense*. Paine's work so impressed General Washington he had it read to the Continental Army for inspiration to stay the course. Paine's pamphlet attacks the bogus "divine right of kings" sovereignty argument as he declared:

"But where, say some, is the King of America? I'll tell you. Friend, he reigns above, and doth not make havoc of mankind like the Royal Brute of Britain. Yet that we may not appear to be defective even in earthly honors, let a day be solemnly set apart for proclaiming the charter; let it be brought forth placed on the divine law, the word of God; let a crown be placed thereon, by which the world may know, that so far as we approve of monarchy, that in America THE LAW IS KING."

That was the thinking of our Founders as they fought the *American War for Life and Liberty* versus the civil government of King George III, and it was the legal argumentation in the Declaration of Independence of 1776.

It is no coincidence that when England diminished the power of the king in their history, they called their new executive "Prime Minister." They learned from the Scriptures that the term *minister* means "to be a servant unto the people." Thus, the chief executive of English

Government was not to be over the people but a servant under the people, protecting their lives and liberty and allowing them to pursue happiness in their **thatched roof castles**. This servant-hood concept carries over into the structure of our **Constitutional Federal Republic**.

In his book *Death By Government*, R. J. Rummel chronicles "the mass murder of their own citizens or those under their protection or control by emperors, kings, sultans, khans, presidents, governors, generals, and others is very much a part of our history." Rummel estimates that in pre-twentieth century world history, there were over 133 million people murdered by government, and in the bloody twentieth century, it was well over 128 million. I bring these horrible historical facts to your attention because it reflects what happens when sinful government leaders are left un-checked and unbalanced, and their powers are not separated but consolidated within a highly, centralized power structure. While the murderous Soviet, North Korean, and Chinese socialists might have called themselves **"Republics,"** they truly represented tyranny as being the exact opposite of our Founders' understanding of liberty in a **Republic under God** and under righteous Law.

While not a perfect nation, the **American Republic** did not join in *democide* or death by government in the twentieth century and was in fact a great liberator from government oppression throughout the world. America is a beacon of righteousness and a shining city upon a hill for the world to see, to flee to, and to be free. The **American Republic** is the greatest living experiment of liberty in the history of the world. When she lives up to her self-evident truths that all men are created equal before the eyes of God and man, she is second to none of all the nations. I mean no disrespect for my country in this book, and anybody who has heard me speak or teach in the last thirty years will attest to the fact that **I love my country, our Republic under God!**

This small book is simply reminding us of where we've been in the eternal war for life and liberty and why we must always be vigilant and suspect of the powers that be. With all the thousands and thousands of books, debates, and technical explanations of the various forms of governments throughout world history, the simple, bottom-line question for us is:

Is the government to be trusted with the power we've given them to protect our life and liberties and to not harm us in our "thatched roof castles"?

History teaches us: No! This little book is an attempt to illustrate historically that even in the great country of America, BIG government has at times violated American citizens' **unalienable castle rights** to life and liberty.

Federal Government – leave us alone!

Suggested Reading:

No, They Can't: Why Government Fails – But Individuals Succeed by John Stossel

Death by Government by R.J. Rummel

Republic, Lost by Lawrence Lessig

CHAPTER 1

THE ACTS OF A GOVERNMENT THAT COULD NOT BE TRUSTED

*The truth is that all men having power ought to be
mistrusted* —James Madison

On October 25, 1760, King George II died, and his grandson George William Frederick became King George III. George III was taught by his mother and court tutors that "an absolute king must rule absolutely" and was also keenly aware of the centuries-old strife that had slowly transferred the absolute power of the Crown to Parliament. From the 1215 Magna Charta that reined in corrupt King John I to the 1649 Cromwellian execution of Charles I to the 1688 Glorious Revolution and the English Bill of Rights, English Law had succeeded in laying the groundwork for the 1775-1783 American Revolution, or what I call the **"American War for Life and Liberty."**

Wars cause DEBT, and the British, French and Indian War that ended in 1763 was no exception to that long-accepted rule. While kings, queens, and nobility may reap the rewards of war through imperial expansion, land acquisition, and the spoils of war, the commoner, the serfs, indentured servants, and the slaves of the kingdom always paid dearly for the foolhardiness of war. If not with their lives, they would certainly pay for the adventures and vainglory of government tyrants with their servitude and the confiscation of the fruits of their labor through taxes and other means.

By 1765 King George III and Parliament declared the Stamp Act or a direct tax on all paper in the Colonies. All documents, letters, newspapers, and licenses had to have an official government "stamp" which cost the colonists money. In effect the Stamp Act meant that no town or village in any colony could do its business without their official papers carrying the King's "stamp." No game of cards could be played; no tavern could operate within the law and ALL marriage licenses had to be stamped with a two-pound duty.

Colonial lawyers and newspaper publishers were especially hurt by this punitive tax. Benjamin Franklin's *Pennsylvania Gazette* was hit hard. Over twenty-two editor-printed newspapers suffered inordinate expenses to pay for the King's War. In an editorial to the *Boston Gazette*, John Adams declared, "They mean to strip us of the means of knowledge!" More and more colonial news-papers began to write on the freedom of the press and speech as the *Connecticut Gazette* announced it would be "the guardian of freedom" and the *Worcester Papers* called for colonial legislatures to "take special care of the LIBERTY OF THE PRESS!"

English colonists felt the British Government had invaded their lives, liberty, and homes in an unprecedented manner. In June of 1765, a number of artisans, tradesmen, shop-keepers, and general laborers in Boston, Massachusetts, organized to challenge the Stamp Act. Eventually, they became known as the *Sons of Liberty*. *Boston Gazette*'s John Gill created a continual flow of public opinion against the egregious, government Stamp Act. Organized under the leadership of a Boston shoemaker, Ebenezer McIntosh, their ranks grew to over two thousand men.

Another leader of the *Sons of Liberty* was Harvard gradu-ate Samuel Adams. Adams' 1743 Master's thesis was titled *Whether it be lawful to resist the supreme magistrate if the commonwealth cannot otherwise be preserved?* Based upon his study of the centuries-old battle between the common man and the kings of England, Adams concluded that after all avenues within reason had been tried, it was the duty of lesser magistrates and the people to resist corrupt supreme magistrates.

As a leader of the Bostonian *Sons of Liberty*, Samuel Adams declared, "If our trade may be taxed, why not our lands? Why not the produce of our lands and everything we possess or make use of? This we apprehend annihilates our charter right to govern and tax ourselves."

By the end of 1765, a *Sons of Liberty* group was created in every colony, and through their utilization of newspapers and pamphlets, more and more colonists were persuaded that the Stamp Act was "unconstitutional." Virginian Patrick Henry presented a number of anti-Stamp Act resolves before the Virginia House of Burgesses in May 1765. He did so not as a radical revolutionary, but he argued legally from within the parameters of the traditional rights of Englishmen. Henry argued that when the King and Parliament imposed the Stamp Act on the Colonies, they violated the "ancient constitution" of England's common law, because they were taxed without proper representation within colonial legislatures.

It is important to note that it would take quite a few more years for loyal, colonial British subjects to even think in terms of a permanent termination of their ancestral, British cultural and legal connections. Our Founders had a profound command of British history and law, and while they despised the tyranny of certain British Monarchs, they admired their British Parliamentary heritage and Monarchs that lived up to their servanthood calling. Initially, they simply wanted the English King and Parliament to respect their ancient chartered rights that were being violated by "unconstitutional innovation." They challenged the British Government, not as revolutionaries but as conservative English traditionalists with a profound respect for the rule of law, arguing from within a British legal framework. That soon would change.

While Parliament rescinded the Stamp Act by 1766, they were not going to let the colonial, upstart tails wag the Parliamentary dogs. They were in charge and were going to make sure the *Sons of Liberty* understood that. In March of 1766 with the King's approval, Parliament passed the Declaratory Act that gave the British Government "full

power and authority to make laws and statutes of sufficient force and validity to bind the Colonies and people
of America, subjects of the crown of Great Britain, in all
cases whatsoever."

Parliament and the King were declaring through "Law"
that Parliament and the King had sovereignty that was
unlimited and un-limitable over the people! To the British
Crown and Parliament, you couldn't divide sovereignty,
but Americans challenged that idea with the sovereignty
of the people, whose ultimate sovereign was King Jesus.
There was an outcry of horror in the Colonies as James
Otis and Sam Adams of Massachusetts, Patrick Henry
and George Mason of Virginia, and many other colonial
leaders were declaring, "Treason! Tyranny!" and "Magna
Charta!" Such Acts, they demanded, destroyed the very
essence of the Judeo-Christian, Anglo-Saxon liberty that
their patriotic British ancestors had fought and died for.
The great Massachusetts lawyer and statesman James Otis
brilliantly laid out the liberty argument by challenging
Parliament's sovereignty, when he declared boldly in court:

> "Parliaments are in all cases to declare what is for
> the good of the whole; but it is not the declaration
> of Parliament that makes it so: There must be in
> every instance, a higher authority – GOD. Should
> an act of Parliament be against any of His natural
> laws, which are immutably true, their declaration
> would be contrary to eternal truth, equity, and jus-
> tice and consequently void."

Notice that word *void* used by Otis. He argues way before 1776 that there might come a time and place when the people have the right to make **null and void** government laws that deny life and liberty.

Pouring salt on an open liberty wound, in 1767 Parliament passed the Townshend Acts or taxes on lead, glass, paper, and tea. The *Sons of Liberty* and colonial legislatures fought the new taxes on many different fronts, which caused the King of England to "invade" the Colonies with British troops in New York and Boston as a show of government arms to intimidate the colonists into submission.

While a number of colonial British subjects were determined to pursue peaceful measures from within British tradition, Samuel Adams, John Hancock, Patrick Henry, and others warned that the British King and Parliament would continue in their unconstitutional measures until all paid homage and duty to the Supreme Magistrate, King George III. In 1773, Parliament passed the Tea Act. While having no new taxes, it was used to bribe compliance with the Townshend Acts and monopolize American merchants.

Led by Samuel Adams and the *Sons of Liberty*, Bostonian Patriots clothed as Indians threw East India Company Tea into the Boston Harbor in December 1773. *Tea Parties* sprouted up all over the Colonies in Annapolis, Maryland, Charleston, South Carolina, and one very interesting one in Edenton, North Carolina, led by Penelope Barker. In October 1774, Penelope hosted a tea party in the home of Elizabeth King, where she called on dozens of female Patriots to sign and follow the boycott of English tea.

She had a copy of her "The Edenton Tea Party Proclamation" printed in a London newspaper, which infuriated London Tories but encouraged women throughout the Colonies to start their own boycotts. In 1775 Haym Salomon, a Polish Jewish immigrant who had established himself in New York City as a brilliant banker and broker for merchants, was involved in the trans-Atlantic trade and decided to join the New York Sons of Liberty. Haym immediately immersed himself in counter British activities, eventually being arrested in September 1776 as a spy and incarcerated for eighteen months on a British ship. He was let go with the agreement he would work as an interpreter for Hessian mercenaries or German soldiers working for England. Salomon convinced a number of Hessians to desert and helped a number of British prisoners escape. When Salomon's covert activities were discovered, he was arrested and tortured in 1778 and sentenced to be hanged, but Haym escaped, fleeing to Philadelphia where he continued his work for the cause of Life and Liberty from the British. It is estimated that Haym Salomon loaned George Washington and the Continental Army the equivalent of nine billion in 2015 dollars. Salomon also financially supported a large number of members of the Continental Congress during their stay in Philadelphia, including James Wilson and James Madison.

By 1784 Salomon's money had run out, and his son petitioned the American Government to repay the money his father had graciously loaned them during the War. They refused. By early 1785 Haym Salomon and his family was penniless, and he died on January 8, 1785, neglected by a government he trusted and dedicated his life to creating. Haym Salomon's life admirably reflects the last line in the Declaration of Independence that declared, "we mutually pledge to each other our Lives, our Fortunes and our sacred Honor." Haym Salomon was truly a patriotic Son of Liberty and a wonderful Founding Father whose life needs to be taught to our children.

Eventually, the economic impact on the British economy infuriated King George III and Parliament. *Tea Parties* and other patriotic activities by the Sons of Liberty caused the British Government to pass a series of laws titled the Coercive Acts, but called by Patriots the "Intolerable Acts."

The Boston Harbor was ordered closed; more British troops occupied Boston, and the government of Massachusetts was now directly under the control of the British Government. The Royal governor was allowed to put royal officials on trial in Great Britain, which George Washington called the "murder act," because it allowed the British to harass and harm Americans and escape justice. Founding Father Richard Henry Lee of Virginia called the Intolerable Acts "a most wicked system for destroying the liberty of America!"

The Crown and Parliament believed their Coercive Acts would divide the *Tea Partiers* and *Sons of Liberty* from the rest of American colonists. It didn't; it backfired, as more and more moderates throughout the Colonies began to join the ranks of those who were declaring with accelerated intensity, "Give me Liberty or give me death!" Out of this unity came the creation in September of 1774 of the First Continental Congress.

On September 6, 1774, the first official act of the Continental Congress was a call to prayer. Why? They were scared. John Adams, Samuel Adams, Patrick Henry, Richard Henry Lee, Roger Sherman, George Washington, and many others from the Colonies understood that the creation of a Continental Congress could lead to war with the world's most powerful empire. In like manner, it is not a coincidence that our First Constitutional Congress in 1789 passed the First Amendment, which begins with "Freedom of Religion" or the right to pray and worship without government control. Christianity and prayer was the lifeblood of liberty-loving Patriots from the beginning of the *War for Life and Liberty* to the creation of our Constitution.

The historic 1774 Continental Congress created the Continental Association, which began to boycott British goods. They also declared that they would stop all exports to Great Britain if they did not stop the Intolerable Acts. The *Republican-Whig* press along with the *Sons of Liberty* propaganda unleashed their editorials against all the King's men, calling on patriotic colonists to join the cause of liberty.

British and American Tories, or those loyal to the King, began a counterattack in the press as expressed by Dr. Seabury who protested, "If I must be enslaved, let it be by a KING at least, and not by a parcel of upstart, lawless committee-men. If I must be devoured, let me be devoured by the jaws of a lion, not gnawed to death by rats and vermin!" Alexander Hamilton, an eighteen-year-old, New York scholar at King's College, replied to Dr. Seabury's Tory sentiments with a brilliant summarization of the ultimate source of Life and Liberty when he wrote:

> "The sacred Rights of Mankind are not to be rummaged for, among old parchments, or musty records. They are written, as with a sunbeam, in the whole volume of human nature, by the Hand of Divinity itself, and can never be erased or obscured by moral power."

The Continental Association agreed that if Massachusetts was attacked by England all the Colonies would join in the War. On April 19, 1775, the British Government attacked the Massachusetts towns of Lexington, Concord, Lincoln, Menotomy, and Cambridge, creating the *American War for Life and Liberty* from a tyrannical, oppressive British Government that had forgotten the "Liberty Legacy" their forefathers had created in the once-great British Parliamentary system.

Between April of 1775 and May of 1776, there continued to be hopes of reconciliation, led by Pennsylvanian Quaker John Dickenson. The tyrannical King George III laughed at their July 1775 *Olive Branch Petition* and increased oppressive legislation and troop occupation in the Colonies. The two most impacting Colonies in the *War for Life and Liberty* were Massachusetts and Virginia with Patriots like Samuel Adams, John Adams, John Hancock, and Patrick Henry, George Mason, and Thomas Jefferson respectively, gearing up for war.

John Adams, the Harvard graduate and lawyer who believed so much in the Rule of Law and due process, had the courage to defend the British soldiers in the 1770 Boston Massacre fiasco. He defended the soldiers brilliantly, causing some to doubt his loyalty to the cause of liberty.

Adams argued that liberty can only be secured through legal means – a proper defense with trial by jury and due process, not mob-rule disregarding evidence. John Adams won his case with brilliant legal acumen, evidence, and a reasoned defense of the British soldiers. While he frustrated many of the *Sons of Liberty*, he gained the respect from those who were warming up to the call for a legal and reasoned argument for "independency" from England. Ironically, within a few years of the massacre trial, John Adams would join his cousin Sam Adams as one of THE main voices for Life and Liberty, and he became a hero to many *Sons of Liberty*.

Suggested Reading:

Samuel Adams: A Life by Ira Stoll

Fighting for Liberty and Virtue by Marvin Olasky

On September 6, 1774, the first official act of the Continental Congress was a call to prayer.

CHAPTER 2

1776 – DECLARING A WAR FOR LIFE & LIBERTY!

When the American spirit was in its youth, the language of America was different: Liberty, sir, was the primary object! —Patrick Henry

By 1776 John Adams had become known as "the voice of Liberty and Independency." On Monday, July 1, 1776, Adams gave a passionate speech before the Second Continental Congress, encouraging his fellow Patriots to sign the Declaration of Independence.

Based upon research that pieced together letters and Adams' recollections as an old man, David McCullough's biography of *John Adams*, and the HBO miniseries of the same name, historians put together his brilliant liberty speech:

"Objects of the most stupendous magnitude.
Measures which will affect the lives of millions –
born and unborn – are now before us. We must
expect a great expense of blood to obtain them,

but we must always remember that a free constitution of civil government cannot be purchased at too dear a rate, as there is nothing on this side of Jerusalem of greater importance to mankind. My worthy colleague from Pennsylvania has spoken with great ingenuity and eloquence. He has given you a grim prognostication of our national future. But where he foresees apocalypse, I see hope. I see a new nation ready to take its place in the world, not an empire, **but a republic. And a republic of laws, not men!** Gentlemen, we are in the very midst of revolution; the most complete, unexpected, and remarkable of any in the history of the world. How few of the human race have ever had an opportunity of choosing a system of government for themselves and their children?

"I am not without apprehensions, gentlemen. But the end we have in sight is more than worth all the means. My belief says that the hour has come. My judgment approves this measure and my whole heart is in it. All that I have, all that I am, and all that I hope in this life I am now ready to stake upon it.

"While I live, let me have a country – **a free country!**"

New Jersey delegate Richard Stockton wrote this of John Adams' contribution to American Liberty:

"Adams was the Atlas of the hour, the man to

whom the country is more indebted for the great measure of independency ... He it was who sustained the debate, and by the force of reasoning demonstrated not only the justice, but the expediency of the measure."

John Adams was a "Patriot Pistol," and like Patrick Henry, he was proclaiming to America and the world that Life and Liberty were worth dying for. While John Adams was known as "the voice of the Declaration of Independence," the Virginian Thomas Jefferson was "The Pen."

In June 1776, the Continental Congress chose John Adams, Roger Sherman, Robert Livingston, Benjamin Franklin, and Thomas Jefferson to draft a declaration of independence. This "Committee of Five" chose Jefferson to write the original draft. When asked by Henry Lee where he got the "revolutionary and new" ideas for the Declaration, Jefferson corrected him by saying, "not to find out new principles, or new arguments, never before thought of ... it was intended to be an expression of the American mind, and to give that expression the proper tone and spirit called for by the occasion."

What did Jefferson mean when he said that in 1776 the Declaration was **"an expression of the American mind?"** Perhaps the answer is found in the suggestion for the original Great Seal of the United States. When Thomas Jefferson, Benjamin Franklin, and John Adams were asked in 1776 to design an original Great Seal of the new "United States," John Adams wrote this to his wife Abigail:

"Mr. Jefferson proposed the children of Israel in

the wilderness, led by a cloud by day, and a pillar
of fire by night, and on the other side Hengist and
Horsa, the Saxon chiefs, from whom we claim the
honor of being descended and whose political principles and form of government we have assumed."

What were the political principles and form of government utilized by the Anglo-Saxon chiefs? Reflecting
the influence of Israelite Mosaic Law and Apostolic New
Testament teaching, they were centuries-old principles of
government by local control, separation of powers, faith-
fulness to limited, enumerated powers with government
leaders, unalienable rights of the individual, and divine
origin of life and liberty.

Jefferson's seal was to be a combination of the Judeo-
Christian and Anglo-Saxon worldview and political principles. Very common in the 1600s and 1700s were political
writings of English and Scottish political philosophers
who had a disdain for Norman tyrants, many of whom
became English tyrannical kings. This "Big government-
Norman yoke" concept was in sharp contrast to the profound admiration for the "limited government liberty"
statutes as practiced and promulgated by the Anglo-Saxons.
Jefferson was especially impressed by the Anglo-Saxon
understanding that their kings were to be "Chief" among
equals. In 1824 Thomas Jefferson wrote to John Cartwright,
a staunch English Whig, "that the difference between the
Whig and the Tory of England is that the Whig deduces
his rights from the Anglo-Saxon source, and the Tory

from the Norman." This same thinking carried over to America's Founders.

Thomas Jefferson penned these glorious words in the Declaration of Independence:

"We hold these truths to be self-evident, that all men are created equal, that they are endowed by their Creator with certain unalienable Rights, that among these are Life, Liberty and the pursuit of Happiness."

According to Michael Patrick Leahy in his excellent book *Covenant of Liberty: The Ideological Origins of the Tea Party Movement,* "Jefferson's famous second paragraph was the perfect blend of Locke, Protestant covenant theology, and the Ancient Constitution, all prepared to throw off the Norman yoke."

That "Norman yoke" from the Norman kings to the Stuart and Hanover Monarchs was to be battled in English and Scottish history for centuries by what became known as *Whigs* and *Republicans.* Obviously, when Jefferson spoke of the "American mind" of 1776, he could not have meant all the American people of 1776. Historians tell us that approximately 25 percent of the colonists were Tories, 25 percent were *Whigs-republicans* (Patriots), and 50 percent were undecided.

Jefferson's "American mind" was in reality the 25-30 percent *Whigs* or *republicans* that early on sided with Life and Liberty versus the tyranny of the British Government. For us to understand the Jeffersonian mind of 1776, we need to understand the *Whig-republican* mind of 1776.

The term *Whig* first appeared in Scotland as a description of the Scottish Presbyterians who fought against the British Government from 1639-1651. These Scots or *Whigs* in the spirit of *Braveheart*'s William Wallace opposed the tyrannical English King Charles I in 1648. *Whigs* were also associated with the Christian Scottish Covenanters who opposed REX LEX (King over the Law) and advocated LEX REX (Law over the King) and *republican* principles. By the late 1600s the British *Whigs* were opposed to the succession of the Catholic King James II. This *Whiggery* was a political philosophy that saw political power stemming first with a sovereign God, then a sovereign people with the government under both. The sovereign people were in covenant or contract with the King or government, and if the King or government violated the servanthood terms of the contract, they had a lawful duty to resist the tyrannical violation of the covenant. These *Whiggish* ideas played a key role in the so-called Glorious Revolution of 1688, where the King's power was diminished and the people's power advanced.

By the 1700s, *Whiggery* ideas became very popular throughout England and in the British Colonies. These ideas were also called *republican* where the colonists claimed to have the same rights as all English citizens, especially stressing the right to be properly represented in the British Parliament. After decades of "intolerable," British Government activities, *Whiggery* or *republicanism* argued for freedom of religion, speech, press, assembly, the right to petition the government, abolition of titles, more frequent elections, economic freedoms, and most importantly, popular sovereignty or the absolute sovereignty of the people over the government, a government that was to be limited, restrained, and accountable to the people.

Exhausted by "Olive Branch" petitioning, American *Whigs* or *republicans* eventually pleaded for the termination of the Intolerable Acts of the British Government while arguing for independence. In 1775 when the *American War for Life and Liberty* began, the term *Whig* was used in reference to any American Patriot colonist who supported independence from Britain. In her classic work on the making of the Declaration of Independence, *American Scripture*, Dr. Pauline Maier writes about the *Whig-republican* view of contract-covenant-compact ideas:

> "Take Rhode Island's revolutionary law of May 4, 1776, which ended that colony's allegiance to the Crown. It began by asserting in good Whig fashion that 'in all states existing by compact, protection and allegiance are reciprocal; the latter being only due in consequence of the former.'"

That Rhode Island May 4, 1776, law declared:

> "We are obliged by necessity, and it becomes our highest duty, to use every means, with which God and nature have furnished us, in support of our invaluable rights and privileges; to oppose that power which is exerted only for our destruction."

Many *Whiggish* and *republican* "declarations" were created by the Colonies during the spring and summer of 1776 when the "American mind" believed it was their obligation and duty to oppose the Intolerable Acts of the British Government in whom they could no longer trust. Many leaders within this group we call our Founding Fathers today were John Adams, John Dickenson, John Hancock, Benjamin Franklin, Samuel Adams, Paul Revere, Nathan Hale, George Washington, and Thomas Jefferson, who always referred to himself as a proud *Whig* or *republican*.

Pulitzer Prize author Joseph J. Ellis in his book *Founding Brothers* writes:

> "The core argument used to discredit the authority of Parliament and the British monarch, the primal source of what were called 'Whig principles,' was an obsessive suspicion of any centralized political power that operated in faraway places beyond the immediate supervision or surveillance of the citizens it claimed to govern. The national government established during the war under the Articles of Confederation accurately embodied the cardinal conviction of revolutionary-era republicanism; namely, that no central authority empowered to coerce or discipline the citizenry was permissible, since it merely duplicated the monarchical and aristocratic principles that the American Revolution had been fought to escape."

That was the 1776 "American mind" Jefferson was referring to in 1824, and that is why the sacred document *The Declaration of Independence* was truly a *whiggish* or *republican* proclamation of Life and Liberty! Those *republican* ideas declared that life and liberty derived from God not government and that our Creator is to be known as He is called in the last paragraph of the Declaration *The Supreme Judge of the world* so that governors and governments in America would always remember that ultimately **it is IN God we trust, NOT the government!**

Thomas Jefferson, the Committee of Five, and the Continental Congress's *republican* values of sovereignty are keenly seen when they declare in the closing paragraph of the Declaration of Independence that the document was ratified by the "Representatives of the united States of America ..." and that the "United Colonies are, and of Right ought to be Free and Independent States ... and Things which Independent States may of right do."

Take note of the small *u* for united above; that is not a typo. Colonial *republican* views on central government were very negative as they experienced the intolerable acts of the British Central Government. Jefferson did not write that the Colonies were a "United State" or a "United States." They were the "united States," with each State acting as a sovereign, independent, political entity. In other words, they were a free and independent country, not an inferior government under a larger central authority. By the end of the *American War for Life and Liberty*, each State had developed a *republican* form of government modeled to a certain degree after the British system minus a king where most power was preserved and executed at the local level. To the "American mind" of the 1776-1789 timeframe,

this *republican* form of government offered the greatest
protection against anarchy and tyranny and could only
survive as long as Americans minimized central government control and adhered to the words declared in 1776
by Samuel Adams at the signing of the Declaration of
Independence:

> "We have this day restored the Sovereign to whom
> all men ought to be obedient. He reigns in heaven
> ... and from the rising to the setting of the sun let
> His kingdom come."

Suggested Readings:

Defending the Declaration by Gary Amos

American Scripture by Pauline Maier

The Constitutional Thought of Thomas Jefferson
by David N. Mayer

CHAPTER 3

A CONSTITUTIONAL FEDERAL REPUBLIC UNDER GOD

We are all Republicans, we are all Federalists
—Thomas Jefferson

As contrasting and volatile as today's political battles and parties can be, there were similar sharp contrasts and at times bitter debates over the size, scope, and role of government in 1787 as our Founders grappled with the adequacies and/or inefficiencies of the united States' first federal constitution, the Articles of Confederation.

Written in the name of "the Great Governor of the World" these articles were designed to create a confederated relationship of thirteen distinct and sovereign States with equal sovereign powers in federal councils with mutual respect by all constituent parts, i.e. **ALL the States**. In the minds of our 1787 Founders, these States were defined as entities on the order of European States such as Spain, France, and England. Article II Section 3 stated, "Each state retains its sovereignty, freedom, and independence, and every power, jurisdiction, and right, which is not by this Confederation expressly delegated to the United States, in Congress assembled."

Eventually, a number of significant figures in the political scene were dissatisfied with what they believed were the inadequacies and weaknesses of the Confederation. From no executive or courts, to inabilities to solve border and commerce disputes, to a lack of monetary cohesiveness or the ability to negotiate treaties with foreign states, these Anti-Confederates eventually took the name *Federalists*.

Through a series of failed attempts to amend the Articles of Confederation, it was agreed to meet in Philadelphia during the summer of 1787 to theoretically amend the weak Articles, not to erase them and start from scratch. This Convention concerned a number of individuals and States. Rhode Island, the smallest State, refused to go. Richard Henry Lee and Patrick Henry from the largest State, Virginia, refused to go with Henry declaring, "I smell a rat!" Samuel Adams, the Father of the *American War for Life and Liberty,* refused to go and wrote in symbolic language to his friend Richard Henry Lee, "I confess, as I enter the building I stumble at the threshold. I meet with a National Government, instead of a Federal union of Sovereign States."

The American ideological divide as expressed by Samuel Adams in 1787 to Richard Henry Lee is with us to this day, and it is divided between two primary camps with nuances along the edges:

One is either **Hamiltonian** in philosophy and practice,

believing in government expansion in action, or one is **Jeffersonian,** believing in government restraint and limitation.

One is either a *Central-Nationalist* or a *Federal-republican.*

The age-old, zillion-dollar question as expressed in the introduction of this book has been:

> **"How much government do we want in America to protect Life and Liberty, and can that government be trusted?"**

We debate that question as vigorously today as they did in 1787.

Here is where it can get tricky with the terminology used in 1787 or in the twenty-first century. Federalists like Alexander Hamilton, John Jay, and James Madison argued with various levels of intensity that the United States needed a true "Federal" system where a central or national power would eliminate the inefficacies of a confederacy. Hamilton was at the extreme spectrum of Federalists, arguing for significantly less State sovereignty and autonomy while calling for a lifetime executive and greater central control.

Madison and Jay toned it down considerably as compared to Hamilton, arguing that a true Federal government would be limited, enumerated, and ultimately under State sovereignty. Or at least that's how it appeared they argued in the ratification process, hoping to convince the States that they had nothing to fear with their proposal of a Federal constitution. When you read Alexander Hamilton's defense of the "Federal" constitution, you are left with a muddled, self-contradictory, discombobulating *Faux-Federalism* or *Fake Federalism.*

So admired by statists today, Alexander Hamilton is what I call a *FINO or* "Federalist In Name Only." Under the guise of Federalism, Hamilton proposed a form of government nothing like that proposed by either *authentic Federalists* or *republicans.* His admiration for the British form of government, which was truly a monarchist worldview, called for a lifetime executive who could veto any legislation, making him the ultimate sovereign and essentially a king. Hamilton's senate would also have lifetime appointments while at times he proposed doing away with State sovereignty by establishing an all-encompassing National government. Hamilton scoffed at the demands by *republicans* for a Bill of Rights, saying the people had nothing to fear from his ideas. Hamilton's ideas show little respect for the Constitution and reveal his disdain for *republicanism* and admiration for a highly centralized national government ruled by elite meritocrats and a lifetime executive.

Like Madison, Hamilton agreed that "men were not angels," but his pessimism on human nature went much deeper, causing him to put more faith in a Hobbesian-Leviathan State to save men from themselves. Unlike Thomas Jefferson, George Mason, Patrick Henry and other *republicans,* Hamilton neglects much of the Medieval Scholastic teaching of the primacy of the person being created in the image of God. Hamilton neglects *republic individualism* for the supremacy of corporate idealism and collectivism of the utopian Rousseau. To Hamilton,

"The State's" power was supreme to secure order; thus the State trumps individual liberties due to their potential to create chaos.

That's why during the Federal government's "War on Whiskey" in 1794 it was natural for Hamilton, in Rousseauian fashion, to lead a militia army of 13,000 men in western Pennsylvania to force men to be free. Unfortunately, Hamilton's Big-government ideas influenced our first and second Presidents, George Washington and John Adams, and they haunt us to this day as practiced in Progressive political philosophy from President Wilson to Barack Obama.

The counter-argument versus Hamilton and the Federalists was led by the "Anti-Federalists." They were not anti-Federal government advocates but more properly called *republicans* or *Federal republicans*. Brilliant minds like George Mason, who refused to sign the Constitution, or Patrick Henry pointed out that there were too many discrepancies, disparities, and lack of specificities when the Federalists explained and defended the so-called true *Federal republican government.*

Elbridge Gerry of Massachusetts remarked very color-fully in 1789 that "those who were called Anti-Federalists at the time complained that they had injustice done them by the title, because they were in favor of a Federal government and the others were in favor of a national one; the Federalists were for ratifying the constitution as it stood, and the others not until amendments were made.

Their names then ought not to have been distinguished by Federalists and Anti-Federalists, but as rats and antirats."

The *antirats'* primary concern during the disputes in the ratification process was whether the proposed constitution would continue to advance popular sovereignty and a State-centered government that the Patriots fought and died for during the *War for Life and Liberty.* The "rats," or Federalists, insisted it would, while *republicans* declared it would not.

It can be argued that the so-called Federalists generally were not true Federalists but Nationalists, putting much more power into the hands of the central government, while the so- called Anti-Federalists or *republicans*, were actually Federalists who wanted an authentic Federal decentralized government that was truly limited, enumerated, separated, checked, and balanced with enough power to protect the people but not too much power to harm life and liberty.

An unfortunate scenario has occurred in our government schools and universities in the last seventy years. This historic scenario says that the Constitution cannot be understood with clarity because it was written long ago when there was no one founding interpretation, and that it is ambiguous and difficult to understand.

Yes it is true there were vigorous debates during and after the Constitutional Convention. Yes, we had extremists like Alexander Hamilton whose statist interpretation did exist, but **the over- all record** is crystal clear. The original understanding and consensus of the intent of our Founders at the Constitutional Convention, the State

Ratification Conventions, and the Bill of Rights Debates profoundly concluded that:

Very few Founders called for a highly centralized National government!

Such an idea was repugnant to them, as that would have violated popular and State sovereignty and to do so would contradict all they had argued and fought for in the *War for Life and Liberty* just a few short years earlier. The overwhelming consensus by both *authentic Federalists* and *republicans* was that government could not be trusted; therefore, it must be limited, local, and restrained from its inevitable nature to hurt and harm the people.

An example of this is the *Son of Liberty*, Samuel Adams. While he did not go to the Constitutional Convention, and like Patrick Henry, "smelled a rat," Adams was an influential delegate to the Massachusetts ratifying convention. Early on Samuel insisted on a Bill of Rights whose omission in the Constitution he considered, like Patrick Henry and George Mason, to be a major flaw. With rigorous debate, he eventually supported the vote to ratify the Constitution but insisted on an *authentic Federal republic*, where the central government was limited and restrained, leaving almost all power to the sovereign people and the States.

That is why it is imperative that one not only studies the debates at the Constitutional Convention but also the long-neglected State Ratification debates and the ratification of the Bill of Rights that sheds enormous light on their passionate desire to establish a *republican form of government* that ultimately puts the people first, then the States, and finally and least, a Federal, decentralized government with a few, VERY few, listed, delineated, and enumerated powers.

From when Delaware, the first State, ratified the Federal Constitution on December 7, 1789, to the last State, Rhode Island, on May 29, 1790, or in December 1791, when Virginia became the eleventh State to ratify the Bill of Rights, we see a reiteration and confirmation that our Founders over and over again called for **LIMITED government**, whose primary purpose was to protect our God-given Life and Liberty and to leave us alone in our **thatched roof castles**.

The Constitution and the Bill of Rights were not ratified as instruments to restrain the people, but on the contrary, they were instruments designed as a *republican form of government* dedicated to retrain the government. By 1789 the Federalists won the Constitutional ratification debate while by 1791 the *republicans* secured the wonderful Ten Amendments dedicated to reminding the Federal government what it cannot and should not do to harm life and liberty.

Suggested Readings:

James Madison and the Making of America
by Kevin R.C. Gutzman

The Federalist: A Commentary on the Constitution of the United States

The Anti-Federalists: Selected Writings and Speeches
edited by Bruce Frohnen

Jake speaking at CPAC-Chicago defending Life & Liberty

CHAPTER 4

GOVERNMENT POWER – FROM WHISKEY TO FREE SPEECH

Government, even in its best state, is but a necessary evil; in its worst state, an intolerable one.

—Thomas Paine

On April 23, 1789, George Washington was sworn in with his hand on the Holy Scriptures as the first President of the United States of America. I have profound admiration for George Washington, who is my all-time favorite President. His integrity, humility, and strength of character in many ways helped not only to create the United States but saved the United States during many dangerous and tumultuous times in our early history. Like most of our Founders, Washington was very suspect of concentrated power in the hands of any government entity. His keen concern over governments' potential harmful effects on life and liberty led him to dedicating his life to the cause of *republican, limited government*, as he believed that "government is not reason, it is not eloquent; it is force. Like fire, it is a dangerous servant and a fearful master."

As a Federalist, George Washington also knew that enough power was necessary to protect the people and that they needed to work out the weaknesses of the earlier Confederation. For the most part, Washington understood the order of the Constitutional power structure as explained in the first three articles of the Constitution. They were never meant to be co-equal branches of government as erroneously taught in junior high American Government classes. Article I, the longest and most detailed, gave the Legislative body, or Congress, the most power, reflecting our Founders' deep reverence for the Rule of Law.

After Congressional prerogative and power came the executive or Presidential power, as laid out in the much shorter Article II of our Constitution. Article III gave the least amount of power to the Judicial Branch, or Federal judges, from the Supreme Court to the lower Federal courts.

With a few notable exceptions, our first five presidents used their power sparingly, issuing only twenty vetoes over legislation deemed unconstitutional by our early executives. Washington vetoed only twice.

One of Washington's notable exceptions was his Whiskey War of 1794. Under the influence of his "FINO" Secretary of Treasury, Alexander Hamilton, Washington's government gravitated towards a more aggressive flexing of central, Federal muscle. Hamilton convinced Washington that to pay for the $80 million war debt with the tyrannical British Government, a 25 percent excise tax on Whiskey at the point of production would not only be a great way to secure significant revenue for the Federal government, but it would let the people and the States know who was ultimately in charge.

Throughout the frontier regions of North and South Carolina, Maryland, Virginia, Kentucky, and western Pennsylvania, citizens declared that not only was the Federal excise tax a burden on their primary source of income, but it was unconstitutional and reminded them of British imperialism where unjust and unlawful taxes were imposed on the people. After the *War for Life and Liberty*, many continued to argue against excise taxes as burdensome. Thomas Jefferson's famous dictum, "That the earth belongs in usufruct to the living," was the *republican* belief that American citizens had the right to receive benefits of the earth and the fruits of their labor without Central government encroachment upon that Liberty.

Republicans argued that only at the most intimate local level could government justly impose an internal tax, because local officials would be more keenly aware of local, cultural, and economic conditions. It was argued that an excise tax imposed by a distant central government would in most cases cause a devastating financial burden on the people and infringe on their lives and liberty.

Resistance to the whiskey tax was widespread with an occasional act of violence against the Federal government. For the most part, the Washington-Hamilton Central government did not have the manpower or will to quash the massive civil disobedience throughout the States, with the exception of western Pennsylvania.

Why was that? In most other whiskey regions, it was

next to impossible to recruit tax collectors, as whiskey was the lifeblood of the region. In reality, the tax was not collected or paid, this being somewhat similar to the colonial hatred of the British Stamp Act of 1765. The other more pragmatic reason by the Federal government was Washington's concerns that the Whiskey War was relatively close to the Capital of the Central government, which was at that time in Philadelphia, Pennsylvania. Both Washington and Hamilton argued that the *republican societies* feeding the flames of this rebellion were influenced by French revolutionary ideas, while those societies argued they were followers of the *republican Sons of Liberty.*

Here's where the predictions of the Anti-Federalists, authentic Federalists or *republicans,* came true. American Revolutionary war hero Thomas Mifflin, the governor of Pennsylvania, did not ask for Federal intervention, nor did the State legislature, and when President Washington led the Federal army invading western Pennsylvania in the summer of 1794, he unconstitutionally violated Article IV, Section 4 which reads:

"The United States shall guarantee to every State in this Union a Republican Form of Government, and shall protect each of them against Invasion ..."

During the Constitutional Convention and Ratification debates, the overwhelming majority of the Founders argued against a Central-Federal army that would violate State sovereignty. Both Thomas Jefferson and James Madison rebuked Hamilton's advice and Washington's actions. It is this rebuke that reflects the serious philosophical divide between the Federalists and *Republicans* in the politics of the 1790s and Presidential Election of 1800 and illustrates the political and philosophical divide in the United States today.

When Thomas Jefferson won the Presidential election of 1800, it reaffirmed the *republican principles* that motivated most of the Founding Fathers of America during the *War for Life and Liberty*. Jefferson's victory practically destroyed the Federalist Party, as it faded away into the sunset during the following decade and led to *republican* administrations of James Madison and James Monroe.

What was it that caused this philosophical and political shift in the land? When President Washington picked Thomas Jefferson as his Secretary of State and Alexander Hamilton as his Secretary of Treasury, little did he know then that he laid the groundwork for the birth of political parties and philosophical government divides that are still with us in America today.

With the blessing of President Washington, the *FINO* Hamilton helped create many new Central government institutions, including the Federal Bank of the United States. This led to Thomas Jefferson's resignation as Secretary of State and aligned more closely the *authentic Federalist* James Madison with the *republican* Thomas Jefferson, as both were profoundly concerned over what they considered to be unconstitutional Central government expansion.

Fearing that an executive who was in office too long would naturally gravitate towards accumulating more power, President Washington decided that two four-year terms were enough for any President to have, thus establishing an executive tradition that held until power-hungry FDR ran for an unprecedented four terms from 1932-1944. Washington's Vice President Federalist John Adams became his successor, narrowly beating *republican* Thomas Jefferson in 1796. Due to the prevailing rules of the Electoral College, Jefferson's votes ironically gave him the Vice Presidency. That would be somewhat comparable to Ronald Reagan being Barak Obama's Vice President or like mixing ammonia and bleach, thus creating poison. Political poison was in Adam's cabinet from the get-go with Jefferson's limited-government, State sovereignty *republicanism* clashing with John Adams' Centralism, censorship, and violations of the Constitution.

Before I proceed to critique John Adams, let me explain my ambivalence over such criticism. No human being is perfect, only God is; thus, even my heroes have flaws, make mistakes, at times make bad decisions, sin and have a propensity, as we all do, to gravitate towards **power**, whether due to insecurity or self-aggrandizement. As stated earlier, "men are not angels, thus the need for government," BUT that is the enigma that is wrapped in a riddle when it comes to the creation of a *republican form of government*.

How much government is enough? I suggest it is in knowing that government is actually people, and that we the people choose less than perfect people to represent us. John Adams, the voice of the Declaration of Independence, a man I admire and whom I call a "Pistol of Patriotism," forgot what he preached to the world in 1776 when he became President in 1797.

There is no President, member of Congress, or Supreme Court justice in our history that has not been guilty of violating somewhere in their political career an improper balance of enough government to protect but not too much government to do harm. While this will never happen, if I were in political office, I too would violate somewhere in my tenure a principle I passionately believed in. This does not excuse the violation but points out the ever-vigilant necessity to guard liberty 24/7/365.

In 1798 Federalists in Congress, along with President Adams' help, argued that stronger Federal laws were needed to protect Americans and American property from potential harm from French ships and French refugees engaged in American politics.

The Federalists accused *republicans* like Vice President Jefferson and *republican* writers and editors of being "French revolutionaries" bringing their pernicious "Reign of Terror" ideas to America. To stop such repugnant *republican* and French ideas, the Federalists passed the Alien and Sedition Acts in 1798, and they were gladly signed by President John Adams. Under the guise of national security, one of the most egregious components of the new Law was that it restricted speech or press that was critical of the Federal government and President John Adams, although it was permissible to attack Vice President Thomas Jefferson. In reality, it was an unconstitutional ploy to destroy their *republican, limited-government* opponents. Over twenty *republican* newspaper editors were arrested, along with dozens and dozens of American citizens with *republican* sentiments. They were either fined or imprisoned for their so-called violation of Federal law.

For instance, David Brown of Dedham, Massachusetts, led a *republican* group to raise a Liberty pole with a sign that declared "No Stamp Act, No Sedition Act, No Alien Bills, No Land Tax, downfall to the Tyrants of America; peace and retirement to the President; Long Live the Vice President." Brown was found guilty of violating the Adams-Federalists, Federal Law, fined $480, and spent eighteen months in prison.

James Thomson Callender, an immigrant from Scotland who had been kicked out of Great Britain for his republican writings, wrote a book that was read and approved by Vice President Thomas Jefferson. In his *The Prospect Before Us,* he criticized President Adams by calling him "a repulsive pedant, a gross hypocrite and an unprincipled oppressor," while declaring the Adams administration a "continual tempest of malignant passions." While writing for the Virginian *Richmond Examiner* in 1800, he was found guilty, fined $200, and spent nine months in jail.

Benjamin Franklin Bache, the editor of the Republican newspaper *Aurora,* attacked Federalist expansion of the Federal government, called George Washington incompetent and John Adams "blind, crippled, toothless, and querulous." Bache was arrested in 1798 but died before his Federal trial.

Republican congressman Matthew Lyon from Vermont

was indicted in 1800 for an essay he wrote where he accused Federalists and the Adams' administration of "ridiculous pomp, foolish adulation, and selfish avarice." Lyon also published *Lyon's Republican Magazine*, subtitled *The Scourge of Aristocracy*, which further enraged his Central government opponents who fined him $1000 and forced him to serve four months in jail. After he served his sentence, he returned to Congress and was praised by *republicans* as a free-speech martyr.

In 1798 Congressman James Madison and Vice President Thomas Jefferson were not only outraged at the Federal government's violation of free citizens' First Amendment rights of freedom of speech and press, they were deeply concerned that the Central government through the Federalists in Congress and President Adams violated the Tenth Amendment. To *republicans* the Tenth Amendment was the foundation of *Federal republicanism*, where a limited Central government left the vast majority of governing to the States as agreed to at the Constitutional Convention and Ratification debates.

To combat this gross violation of Constitutional law, Madison and Jefferson drafted the *Virginia* and *Kentucky Resolutions* that declared "states, in contesting obnoxious laws, should 'interpose for arresting the progress of the evil'" and "that the several States who formed that instrument being sovereign and independent, have the unquestionable right to judge of its infraction; and that a Nullification by those sovereignties, of all unauthorized acts done under color of that instrument is the rightful remedy ... "

Jefferson's Constitutional "whigism" was predicated according to David N. Mayer "on a profound distrust of concentrated political power and, with it, an especially intense devotion to the ideal of limited government." That is why in his 1798 Kentucky Resolutions he declared:

> "Confidence is everywhere the parent of despotism-free government is founded in jealousy, and not in confidence; it is jealousy and not confidence which prescribes limited constitutions, to bind down those whom we are obliged to trust to power ... In question of powers, then, let no more be heard of confidence in man, but bind him down from mischief by the chains of the Constitution."

Madison and Jefferson were reminding the Federal government of their Federal contract. As expressed in the Constitution, they were granted a few enumerated powers in comparison to the sovereign States, and when the Federal government violated that contract or covenant, the States were obligated to make null and void unconstitutional acts as expressed in the Federal Alien and Sedition Acts.

While it is true that a number of *republicans* believed the Kentucky and Virginia Resolutions went too far in calling for State governments to invalidate Federal laws establishing the potential for State sedition, they laid the legal argument for the ultimate question our Founders debated time and time again:

Who was the ultimate sovereign authority and who created whom and what do you do when all three branches of the Federal government violate Life and Liberty?

In other words, what do you do when the Federal Fox is guarding the Liberty chicken coop of popular and State sovereignty?

Was that not the ultimate question asked by our Founders in 1776 when declaring independence from the tyrannical British Government, and was that not the ultimate question debated at the Constitutional and Ratification debates?

Well of course it was! What do you do when **every branch** of the Federal government is hostile to Life and Liberty? You fight it!

In an authentic Federal system, the Federal government is not the only player in the game of government. State governments are to have a major role; in fact, they, along with the people, were to play **THE major role in government!**

Jefferson's understanding of *Federal republicanism* was "that barriers or our liberty in this country are our State governments." His ideas were not just mere abstractions but clearly laid out in the 1798 Kentucky Resolutions. Jefferson understood that the new *Federal republic* would establish its unique personality early on; therefore, it must be watched and critiqued like a hawk. Because *republican* allies of Jefferson were being arrested and jailed, some feared that even Vice President Jefferson might be charged with sedition and jailed; therefore, James Madison, Thomas Jefferson and other *republican* leaders met in secret to draw up a strategy and write a defense of *Life and Liberty* versus the Federal government.

This Jefferson-Madison strategy, known today as the

Principles of 98, was a clear and cohesive understanding by two major Founding Fathers of *Federalism* and the proper relationship between a limited Central government and the key component of a *Federal Republic*: **the States**.

Jefferson wrote the Kentucky Resolutions using an intermediary to introduce them in the legislature. Jefferson's major premise was that in Federalism the Union was a compact among the States with the thirteen sovereign States composing the *united States of America*, which according to him:

> "Are not united on the principle of unlimited submission to their General Government ... by compact under the style and title of a Constitution for the United States ... they constituted a General Government for special purposes, delegated to that government certain definite powers, reserving, each State to itself, the residuary mass of right to their own self-government."

According to David Mayer in his excellent book *The Constitutional Thought of Thomas Jefferson*:

> "From this general theory of the Union, Jefferson derived two basic corollary principles. First, since it was created by the compact for special, limited purposes only, 'whensoever the General Government assumes undelegated powers, its acts are unauthoritative, void, and of no force.' Second, the government created by the compact could not be 'the exclusive or final judge of the extent of the

powers delegated to itself because that would have made its discretion, and not the Constitution, the measure of its powers ... as in all cases of compact among powers having no common judge each party (that is, each state) has an equal right to judge for itself, as well of infractions as the mode and measure of redress.'"

Jefferson and many *republicans* were alarmed at the blatant unconstitutional and partisan tyranny displayed by the general government, which they felt was not exercising true, restrained Federalism but an ever-expanding Centralism, or what we call today Statism. Due to this Federal monopoly, Jefferson and the *republicans* strategized to "take a stand in the State legislatures," which to them was the proper place for State sovereignty to defend liberty over the **tyranny of an unbalanced Federal government**.

Thus Jefferson concluded in his Kentucky Resolutions "that each individual state has the power to declare that federal laws are unconstitutional and void. The Kentucky Resolution of 1799 added that when the states determine that a law is unconstitutional, nullification by the states is the proper remedy."

In like manner James Madison wrote the Virginia Resolutions which started out by declaring that the sovereign State of Virginia would "maintain and defend the Constitution of the United States, and the Constitution of this state, against every aggression, either foreign or domestic." Madison was expressing a proper and balanced Federalism that gave respect to the Federal Constitution but gave the utmost deference to the Virginia State Constitution. The essence of Madison's challenge to the Federal centralistic and tyrannical Alien and Sedition Acts is reflected in this key passage from the Virginia Resolution:

> "That this Assembly doth explicitly and peremptorily declare, that it views the powers of the federal government, as resulting from the compact, to which the states are parties; as limited by the plain sense and intention of the instrument constituting the compact; as no further valid that they are authorized by the grants enumerated in that compact; and that, in case of a deliberate, palpable, and dangerous exercise of other powers, not granted by the said compact, the states who are parties thereto, have the right, and are in duty bound, to interpose for arresting the progress of the evil, and for maintaining within their respective limits, the authorities, rights and liberties appertaining to them."

Madison's resolution went on to decry the Federal government's expansion and perpetuation of its own powers at the expense of State sovereignty and that the continuation of this legislative, executive, and judicial behavior would lead to the demise of true *Federal republican* government in America.

Madison was so concerned about Federal power that he came out of retirement to enter the Virginia Assembly, and wrote the *Virginia Report of 1800.* In that report he not only elaborated on *republican constitutional principles,* but he reiterated his critique of the Big-government Alien and Sedition Acts. Madison attacked the Federalist dominance of the Federal government and their violations of true *Federal republican principles.*

A key issue in his report was with the Federalists' use and definition of the word *state*. Federalists like Hamilton and Adams rejected the idea that "the states had created the federal government." In his excellent book *James Madison and the Making of America*, Kevin R. C. Gutzman summarizes Madison's "state" issue by writing:

> "The most common state criticisms of the Virginia and Kentucky resolutions asserted that the state legislatures had no rightful role in interpreting the U.S. Constitution and that the people, not the states, had created the federal government. In regard to the latter, Madison explained what his opponents must surely have known: that the word *states* had different meanings. One might use the word *state* in reference to the territory of a state, as in: Tomorrow I'm going to the state of New York. Alternatively, one might use the word *state* in reference to the government, as in: The state of Connecticut taxes people to support the Congregational church. The third definition was crucial. It referred to the sovereign people of a state, as in: The state of Virginia ratified the Constitution. Madison said that it was in this sense that *Republicans* claimed the states had ratified the Constitution. The fact was indisputable."

Republicans clearly understood that the Union was a federation of sovereign peoples: the people of Massachusetts, the people of North Carolina, the people of Rhode Island, the people of Virginia, and they created a Federal *republican form of government* that was to be very limited in its powers with most power at the feet of the people and the States. *Republicans* rightfully rejected the Nationalist, Centrist, and Monarchist interpretation and distortion of true Federalism in relationship to life and liberty.

While Jefferson and Madison's "1798 Resolutions" and other *republican* writings did not establish a checkmate on Federal usurpation of State sovereignty, it did slow it down and reiterated the reality of a proper and balanced Federalism in relationship to life and liberty. Growing concerned over the Federalist overreach, the American people elected Thomas Jefferson President in 1800, while James Madison became his right-hand man as Secretary of State. For the next twenty-four years, *republicanism* overall would run the country.

Before we explore government in the United States in relationship to slavery and life and liberty, I want to address the issue of James Madison's government worldview. Called the Father of the Constitution in his lifetime, a title he rejected with all humility, Madison is at times all over the place between the Federalists and the republicans on the size and scope of the Federal government. To historians he is sometimes a Nationalist in the direction of the *FINO* Hamilton, and then at other times a *true republican* aligning with Jefferson due to his fear of too strong of a Central government.

I believe Madison is a prime example of the strong desire to limit central government so as not to harm life and liberty but at the same time wanting enough central government to establish an effective *republican form of government* that protects life and liberty. Philosophically Madison had an incredible swing going from pleading at the Constitutional Convention that the Federal government should have veto power over State laws and then joining with Jefferson when he felt the Federal government's Alien and Sedition Acts violated the Tenth Amendment.

His experience with a weak Central government during the War of 1812 caused him as President of the United States to change his thinking and actions to again support a stronger navy, standing army, a national bank, and more Federal control over states, thereby rejecting his earlier nullification position he held with Thomas Jefferson. The struggles Madison experienced from the 1780s until the 1820s are the struggles we face in America today. With James Madison's dilemma in mind, I ask the zillion-dollar question again:

How much government is necessary and can it be trusted?

This much we do know: While there is much to be proud of with the early years of the American Republic, there was an albatross of tyranny that plagued the land. **It was the plague of Slavery**, a plague that reflected once again government's cancerous desire to eat away at the sacredness of life and liberty. This Big-government plague occurred at both the Federal and State level. That is our next story: how two forces of government within our Federal Republic eventually led to America's costliest and bloodiest war, our Civil War.

Suggested Readings:

The Founding Fathers Guide to the Constitution
by Brian McClanahan

The Politically Incorrect Guide to the Constitution
by Kevin Gutzman

The Heritage Guide to the Constitution
Edited by Edwin Meese III

CHAPTER 5

SLAVERY & DEATH BY FEDERAL & STATE GOVERNMENTS

Our Confederate Republic ... is founded ... upon the great truth that the negro is not equal to the white man —Alexander Stephens, Vice-President of the Confederate States of America

Not all government and all of our Founders were guilty of perpetuating the enslavement of people in our founding years. In a 2008 speech on race, President Barack Obama (Obama was a Senator when he gave that speech) declared that the Declaration of Independence was "stained by this nation's original sin of slavery." Actually as a "Nation," we were divided over the issue for over two centuries. Yes, there was sin, but like the divide by our Founders over how much government to have, there was passionate and heated debate over the issue of slavery. Many critics of America's Founding Fathers say they all were advocates and practitioners of slavery and full of hypocrisy when they declared, "all men were created equal" and yet owned slaves. While it is true some Founders were advocates and practitioners of slavery, the historical record is much more complicated than that.

Slavery was introduced in America two hundred years before 1787, and it was not until our Founders came along that there was a serious effort to end slavery in the land. The *American War for Life and Liberty* brought a new antislavery awareness and positive attitude to the idea that "all men were created equal." It was our Founders who laid the foundation for the termination of slavery within a few generations of the birth of the United States. In reality there was the good, the bad, and the ugly when it came to what government did to advance slavery, as well as to terminate slavery in America. That government struggle led to our bloody *Civil War for Life, Liberty and the end of Slavery*.

First the good. In the 1780's Benjamin Rush and Benjamin Franklin founded the first abolitionist society in Pennsylvania. Our first Supreme Court Chief Justice, John Jay, was the president of the New York antislavery society. Many other prominent Founders were members of abolitionist societies, namely James Madison, James Monroe, William Few, John Marshall, Richard Bassett, Richard Stockton, Zephaniah Swift, James Wilson, John Witherspoon, and many more. John Adams passionately hated slavery and proudly declared that he "never owned a slave."

Due to these Founders' efforts, State governments in Massachusetts and Pennsylvania ended slavery in 1780; Rhode Island and Connecticut in 1784; New Hampshire in 1792; Vermont in 1793; New York in 1799; and New

Jersey in 1804. Additionally, the Federal government under President George Washington and our first Congress prohibited slavery in the Northwest Territories that eventually became the States of Illinois, Indiana, Michigan, Ohio, and Wisconsin. This Federal law, called the Northwest Ordinance, was signed into law by President Washington who had stated, "I can only say that there is not a man living who wishes more sincerely than I do to see a plan adopted for the abolition of slavery."

During the Constitutional Convention, there were a number of Founders who wanted to end slavery immediately, but due to adamant opposition by slavery advocates with threats to leave the Convention, many compromises were created. One such compromise is the much- misunderstood, so-called pro-slavery, **three-fifths clause** of the Constitution. The historical record of the Constitutional Convention shows that this clause was actually anti-slavery and wisely added to our Constitution to reduce slavery in the United States. Doctor Walter Williams explains:

> "It was slavery's opponents who succeeded in restricting the political power of the South by allowing them to count only three-fifths of their slave population in determining the number of congressional representatives. The three-fifths of a vote provision applied only to slaves, not to free blacks in either the North or South."

The three-fifths clause was an attempt to reduce the number of pro-slavery advocates in Congress. By reducing the slave count from one to three-fifths, Southern States were actually being denied more pro-slavery representatives in Congress. Unfortunately, even with the significant majority of Founders who were opposed to slavery, by creating State and Federal laws that were designed to eradicate that evil from the land, there were some Founders from the South, such as North and South Carolina and Georgia, who worked to preserve and advance slavery.

Now to the bad and ugly. Do you remember earlier when I asked the question, **"What do you do when the Federal Fox is guarding the Liberty chicken coop of popular and State sovereignty?"**

When discussing Federalism, States' Rights, slavery, or the American Civil War, we get a plethora of opinions, interpretations, and schools of thought. Some people declare that Abraham Lincoln was a Big-government tyrant who disregarded the Constitution, while others consider him a savior and liberator who lived up to the glorious words of the Declaration of Independence and understood the Constitution like no other president since Thomas Jefferson.

One can get a confused understanding of what was really going on when it came to the relationship between the Federal government, State governments, and slavery. There are plenty of books on the legitimacy or illegitimacy of the Federal government's involvement in the Civil War and Abraham Lincoln's culpability or sainthood in relationship to that War.

This little book does not address those issues directly or in depth, but if you want to study Lincoln and slavery,

I recommend Thomas DiLorenzo's *The Real Lincoln* and the contrasting book *Vindicating Lincoln* by Thomas L. Krannawitter. However, I do want to clear the air on the "Slavery-States' Rights" situation before the Civil War and how that connects to *authentic Federalism*.

The concept of federalism and States' rights, where there is the idea of divided power between central and local units, is found in much of world history, especially in Western civilization. Due to their mistrust of highly centralized government when Thomas Jefferson, George Mason, Patrick Henry, James Madison, and others created a *Federal Republic*, they understood that *Federalism* was primarily a **de-centralizing** form of government, where the emphasis for power lay with the people at local and State levels and the central or Federal government was last in position of power in most governance.

That is why as explained earlier there were profound and passionate debates over making sure that they properly defined, delineated, and explained in no uncertain terms what Federalism was, and as a *republican form of government* the people and the States were guaranteed the most power for life and liberty. Without that overwhelming consensus and understanding, the Constitution would have never been ratified and accepted by the people and the States, as they made up the new *Federal Republic*.

We hear people talk about States' Rights or Tenth Amendment Rights, when in reality we need to think in terms of authentic *Federalism* as understood by our

Founders. Far too often we find contradictory explanations of States' Rights and Federalism in relationship to Slavery. Try not to get confused as we explain how the government powers were schizophrenic and all over the place on this issue. Earlier I explained how Northern States passed laws ending slavery, and the Federal government in 1789 created a few laws to that end also. Unfortunately, the doubled-minded Federal government passed the Fugitive Slave Law in 1793, where the Federal government gave power to local authorities in both Slave and Free States to recapture any Negro they thought to be an escaped slave. In 1808 they abolished the Slave trade as agreed to at the Constitutional convention as a compromise. Then in 1819 they allowed Missouri to enter the Union as a Slave State and in 1820 Maine as a Free State. They called it a "compromise," but in reality the Federal government was complicit in the advancement of Slavery, the very antithesis of the Declaration of Independence.

Through the influence of the young Democrat party, the Southern States invoked their sovereignty to work around the 1808 Federal termination of the slave trade by passing more and more State laws insuring the preservation and perpetuation of Slavery.

Eventually, Democrats controlled not only Southern State governments but began to have a profound influence on the Federal government from 1830 to 1860. In 1850 the Democrat- controlled Federal government passed a modified and more egregious version of the 1793 Fugitive Slave Law, where slaves could not testify on their own behalf, and Federal commissioners and agents were used to force Northern States to return escaped slaves. The Federal government was in reality kidnapping free Americans of African heritage. The very same Federal government Democrats, who earlier in the name of States' Rights bemoaned Federal government laws against slavery, were now hypocritically denying and violating Northern States' Rights.

See how confusing this can get.

By 1854 Federal government Democrats passed the Kansas-Nebraska Act, which advanced slavery into new territories. Then in 1857 the democratically controlled, Federal Supreme Court passed the dreadful Dred Scott Decision declaring that an American African Slave was not a citizen or a person but equal to property such as a pig or a cow. By 1860 not only had Southern States entrenched slavery in the South through Democrat State government, but the Federal government controlled by Democrats had advanced and entrenched slavery throughout much of southern and western America.

Both **State and Federal** Government were working hard to enslave human beings. This was not authentic *Federalism* or a *Federal Republic* predicated on and dedicated to the self-evident truth that all men were created equal. **This was anti-liberty tyranny by BOTH forms of Government!**

It is true that in 1798 Jefferson and Madison passed resolutions that challenged constitutional violations of the First and Tenth Amendments by calling for the nullification

of Federal law but they never advocated using these resolutions to advance slavery.

When South Carolina's John C. Calhoun invoked
nullification in 1832, he did so to protest Federal tariffs
he thought were unconstitutional and only backed down
when Democrat President Andrew Jackson threatened to
invade South Carolina with Federal troops.

Here's the irony that is almost always ignored by the
so-called, States' Rights advocates: **It was Northern States
that invoked nullification in their "War for Life and
Liberty" to end slavery that angered Federal and State
Southern Democrats!**

South Carolina's *Declaration of the Immediate Causes
Which Induce and Justify the Secession of South Carolina
from the Federal Union* angrily declared:

> "The States of Maine, New Hampshire, Vermont,
> Massachusetts, Connecticut, Rhode Island, New
> York, Pennsylvania, Illinois, Indiana, Michigan,
> Wisconsin and Iowa, have enacted laws which
> either **nullify** the Acts of Congress or render use-
> less any attempt to execute them."

Notice that word *nullify.* Southern States were furious
with the Northern government or States exercising their
rights to defend life and liberty; thus, they rebelled against
an *authentic Federalism* that advanced life and liberty and
did not perpetuate slavery. South Carolina, the leader of
the rebellious slave States, attacked the State of New York
when they chose to freely exercise their State sovereignty

by declaring that any slave brought into New York would become free. South Carolina was additionally furious when a number of Northern States exercised their sovereignty by allowing American males of African ancestry the right to vote. In 1860 South Carolina invoked the Federal Constitution and the 1857 Federal Dred Scott Decision by declaring that according to "the supreme law of the land [Negroes] are incapable of becoming citizens."

Southern States were also offended that Northern and Western States "denounced as sinful the institution of slavery" and allowed for abolitionist societies to freely express their disdain for slavery and desire to see it eradicated from America. In the 1830s, Southern States created the Gag Rule in an attempt to shut down open debate in Congress and passed measures to destroy freedom of speech, press, and assembly. Postmasters refused to deliver abolitionist literature, and most slave States declared public, anti-slavery speech a criminal offense.

The South was not defending States' Rights and *limited republican government* against a tyrannical Federal government. The South did not rebel against the Federal government in 1860 and 1861 in order to advance "republicanism, equal protection of equal rights, and government by consent within its boundaries; it seceded to secure the Southern way of life, a way of life that revolved in many ways around the institution of human slavery ..."

Southern States' Rights advocates ignored Southern Founding Fathers like George Mason, Thomas Jefferson, Patrick Henry, and James Madison, who understood the inextricable connection between *republicanism,* justice, and freedom of expression. In a *republic* that revered freedom of speech, immoral institutions like slavery would be openly criticized, as our Founders believed freedom of inquiry through speech would peaceably persuade citizens of the need to eliminate it from the land.

But the Southern slave States could not be reasoned with. Mississippi's *Declaration of the Immediate Causes* declared, "Our position is thoroughly identified with the institution of slavery, the greatest material interest of the world."

Southern States' perverted understanding of *Federalism* caused them to rebel against life and liberty so they could create "the world's first Slave Nation!" On March 21, 1861, in Savannah, Georgia, the Vice President of the Confederacy, Alexander Stevens, proudly declared in his infamous and anti-liberty *Confederate Cornerstone Speech*:

> "Our Confederate Republic ... is passing through one of the greatest revolutions in the annals of the world. Seven States have within the last three months thrown off an old government and formed a new ... Our new government is founded upon exactly the opposite idea; its foundations are laid, its cornerstone rests, upon the great truth that the negro is not equal to the white man; that slavery, subordination to the superior race, is his natural and normal condition. This, our new government, is the first, in the history of the world, based

upon this great physical, philosophical, and moral truth."

Thank God Alexander Stephens' Confederate "Slave State Nation" was defeated in 1865!

I am proud to say that in my home State of Wisconsin our Supreme Court in 1859 called for the nullification of the evil Federal Fugitive Slave Act when they defended a Wisconsin citizen's right to defend a runaway slave by the name of Joshua Glover. Abolitionist Sherman Booth helped rescue a Federal government-kidnapped Joshua Glover from Federal custody in a Milwaukee, Wisconsin, jail in 1854. Glover made it to freedom in Canada, while Booth was thrown in a Federal prison. The Wisconsin Supreme Court ordered Booth released and declared the Federal government's Fugitive Slave Act of 1850 unconstitutional and a violation of State sovereignty. The Wisconsin State Historical Society summarizes Joshua's story on a Milwaukee historical marker by saying:

> "Joshua Glover was a runaway slave who sought freedom in Racine in 1852. In 1854, his Missouri owner used the Fugitive Slave Act to apprehend him. This 1850 law permitted slave catchers to cross State lines to capture escaped slaves. Glover was taken to Milwaukee and imprisoned.

> "Word spread about Glover's incarceration and a great crowd gathered around the jail demanding his release. They beat down the jail door and released Joshua Glover. He was eventually escorted to Canada and safety.

"The Glover incident helped galvanize abolitionist sentiment in Wisconsin. This case eventually
led the state supreme court to defy the federal
government by declaring the Fugitive Slave Act
unconstitutional."

Notice the very last sentence of this historical marker.
**"This case eventually led the state supreme court to defy
the federal government by declaring the Fugitive Slave
Act unconstitutional."**

This was a sovereign Northern State defying the Federal
government's advancement of slavery and denial of liberty!
The State of Wisconsin got the constitutional and legal idea
from James Otis when he declared in the 1760s that an act
of Parliament that defied God's Law should be made **void.**
And Wisconsin was profoundly influenced by Thomas
Jefferson and James Madison's "Principles of 98" which,
as stated earlier, were a clear and cohesive understanding
by two major Founding Fathers of Federalism and the
proper relationship between the limited Central government and the KEY component of a *Federal Republic*: **The
people and The States.**

Unfortunately, the anti-liberty Federal Supreme Court
ignored the thinking of Otis, Jefferson, and Madison and
declared that the Wisconsin Supreme Court was out of
line and had no authority to nullify Federal Law. Sherman
Booth's lawyer, Wisconsin Republican activist Carl Schurz,
made this very accurate statement about the clash with
the Federal government and the State of Wisconsin when
he said:

"The Republican Party went to the very verge
of Nullification, while the Democratic Party ...
became an ardent defender of Federal Power."

How ironic and hypocritical. We are told by so-called,
States' Rights advocates that the Civil War was primarily
about the sovereignty of Slave-State Rights, and yet when
the Southern States saw Northern States exercise their
State sovereignty for the defense of Liberty against a life
and liberty-killing Federal government, they declared
"Foul-Federal power over the States!"

In their passionate and bloody desire to preserve and
perpetuate slavery, not only did they deny Northern State
sovereignty for liberty, they were for the advancement of
a corrupt Federal government's advocacy of a "Slave State
Nation."

The birth of the anti-slavery Republican Party in 1854
and their eventual 1860 ascension into the Federal government challenged the Democrat, Central government,
slavery status quo. Thus, the Democrat Slave States aban-
doned the Federal government, declaring a Confederate
Slave State Nation. On April 12, 1861, they attacked the
Federal government that was by then on a course to terminate Slavery and advance liberty throughout the land.

Remember Wisconsin Republican Carl Schurz, the
lawyer who defended Sherman Booth, the liberator of
Joshua Glover in 1854? He summarized the whole convoluted mess of the hypocrisy of the Federal government
and Slave State Rights when he stated:

"In the North, as well as in the South, men's

sympathies with regard to slavery shaped and
changed their political doctrines and their constitutional theories. In the South, it was State-Rights
or the supremacy of the Federal power, as the one
or the other furthered the interest of slavery; in the
North, it was State-Rights or the supremacy of the
Federal power, as one or the other furthered the
interest of freedom."

In his masterful book *Vindicating Lincoln*, Thomas
L. Krannawitter summarized how slavery was the key to
Southern States going to war to preserve slavery and not
States' Rights:

> "The Civil War erupted because the South refused
> to accept the results of the 1860 presidential elec-
> tion, although it had been conducted in strict
> conformity with the rules of the Constitution.
> The cause of the Confederacy was not the cause
> of limited government or states' rights. Slavery
> represented the ultimate rejection of limited
> government. Allowing slavery to spread without
> restriction, as Southerners demanded at the 1860
> Democratic convention, was not spreading limited
> government; it was spreading despotism. Yet, the
> South demanded not only that slavery be allowed
> to spread but that its spread be protected by an
> unprecedented expansion of federal power."

Hypocritically, the defenders of Southern States' Rights
declare that Abraham Lincoln's Federalism was tyranny

against Southern States, while they conveniently ignore that in reality the so-called, limited-government Confederacy ruled by tyrannical Big government dictates all throughout the South. Democrat President Jefferson Davis and the Democrat Confederate Congress passed laws that ran roughshod over States' Rights by fixing prices, seizing property, making arbitrary arrests, controlling labor and transportation, and establishing a huge central government bureaucracy that violated Southern civil liberties and resembled nothing close to a so-called confederacy. This was all done in the name of States' Rights, limited government, and the perpetuation of slavery. Thank God they lost!

The Republicans were responsible for what have become known has the "Civil War Amendments" – the Thirteenth, Fourteenth and Fifteenth Amendments ending slavery, State discrimination, and allowing all American males of age the right to vote. In Steven Spielberg's movie *Lincoln*, you see a determined Abraham Lincoln working tirelessly to get a small number of Democrats to vote with Republicans on the Thirteenth Amendment outlawing slavery in America. I love this line from the Republican Fourteenth Amendment, Section 1 where it states: "Nor shall any State deprive any person of life, liberty, or property without due process of law ..."

The Thirteenth, Fourteenth, and Fifteenth Amendments express a Federal government correcting itself and making amends by advancing liberty over the tyranny of the Federal government and Southern States of pre-Civil War years. Unfortunately, once the Republicans left the South in the late 1870s, the Southern State governments turned to their old, tyrannical, racist ways and began to terrorize through Democrat organizations like the Ku Klux Klan, Red Shirts, and the Knights of the White Camellia Negros. The Southern State governments encouraged these groups and sympathetic whites into either disengaging in the democratic process or engaging in passing racist State laws that ignored the Federal 14th and 15th Amendments. Vile "Jim Crow" Laws were alive in Southern State governments while once again Life and Liberty was dying in Dixie until both Republicans and Democrats in the 1950s and 60s would challenge the bogus anti-liberty "States' Rights" argument that violated the sovereignty of southern citizens.

I don't care what expression or branch of government it is, Federal, State, Legislative, Executive, Judicial, County, City, Town, or Village:

NO government has a right to deny any person life, liberty, or property without due process that upholds the rule of righteous law. Here is how the Fourteenth Amendment should read:

> **"Nor shall any Government, State or Federal, deprive any person of life, liberty, or property without due process."**

Fortunately, there were times when the Federal government acted properly and defended liberty, and there were times when the States defended liberty versus slavery. But unfortunately, there were far too many times when both

Federal and State governments failed to protect life and liberty but acted in tyranny in relationship to slavery and liberty.

Our Founders' vision was a *republican form of government* that established enough power to protect liberty, while at the same time checking that power at all levels to insure that it did not destroy liberty. How soon the *Federal republican* government forgot what a true Federal government was all about! It was supposed to be about Life and Liberty, not the advancement of slavery. And it took a horrible war to fix it.

Sadly, the racist, hateful, and stubborn Democrat Slave States would not let go of their love of slavery, and this Slave State hatred and denial of true *republican*, liberty-loving principles created a horrible *Civil War for Life and Liberty,* or as stated by John Quincy Adams in the movie *Amistad,* the "last Battle of the American Revolution."

Suggested Readings:

American History in Black & White
by David Barton

Southern Rights: Political Prisoners and the Myth of Confederate Constitutionalism by Mark E. Neely, Jr.

The Confederate and Neo-Confederate Reader: The "Great Truth" about the "Lost Cause."
Edited by James W. Loewen and Edward H. Sebesta

Jake in Green Bay, WI defending Religious Freedom vs. Obamacare!

CHAPTER 6

1913 to TODAY – PROGRESSIVISM VERSUS OUR FEDERAL REPUBLIC

A great democracy has got to be progressive or it will soon cease to be great or a democracy.

—Theodore Roosevelt

How wrong Teddy Roosevelt was! America is a Republic under God, not a Progressive Democracy under Government.

—Jake Jacobs

The Democrat Party's defense of slavery and denial of authentic *republican*, liberty principles is a classic example of enslavement and death by a government that could not be trusted. However, in spite of that dark side of American history, the overarching reality is that our Founders' *Federal Republic* has been a resounding *Life and Liberty* success story!

On many, many different fronts, millions of Americans were living in freedom and prosperity from 1787 to 1913 without government encroachment in their lives. Due to hardened hearts when State and Federal governments denied life and liberty, an unfortunate but necessary Civil War was fought to terminate slavery and advance liberty. The beauty of our *Republic under God* is that while it is not perfect, it has a righteous standard to guide it as expressed in the Declaration of Independence and Constitution. When properly applied, this guide gives our government leaders a standard by which to measure the government's ability to fulfill its mission of protecting life and liberty. Fortunately, our Founders blessed us with a *republican form of government* that is a self-correcting system IF the people work in tandem with their representatives to ensure that life and liberty are always protected in the land. This is a constant battle that demands vigilance on the part of the citizens and righteous representatives, because government forces are always at odds with limiting itself. All in all, our *Federal republican*, grand experiment has been an exceptional example of how a government can be limited if the people are willing to pay the price for their liberty. It was Benjamin Franklin who quipped, "Those who give up essential liberty to purchase a little temporary safety deserve neither liberty nor security."

That desire for security over liberty began its creeping ways into the fabric of American society in the year 1913, as a relatively small, limited Federal government. This limited government would begin to die a slow death as a larger, unlimited, and all-encompassing Federal government "progressed" its way into American lives like never before.

All thanks to the anti-constitutional, *progressive* Woodrow Wilson and his protégé Franklin Delano Roosevelt.

Generally speaking, our *Republic* was a limited-government success between 1789 and 1913. Yes, I know we can find a number of examples of the ancient battle between liberty of the individual and The State, some of which we have pointed out in this book. We also expressed in the previous chapter the ugly advancement of slavery and the denial of life and liberty for Americans of African ancestry by government forces at the State and Federal levels. However, overall the central government remained relatively small in comparison to American liberty.

I have reiterated and stressed throughout this book that originally our Federal government was a *republic*, where we the people in covenant or contract with them allowed them to have a **few**, I repeat a few, enumerated and **very limited** powers as explicitly and specifically spelled out in our Constitution. These very few powers were designed to protect us from harm by the government and **NEVER** did we grant them unlimited powers that would destroy the very essence of life and liberty!

Unfortunately, all that changed around the turn of the nineteenth century with the arrival and permeation of Fabian socialists, cultural and militant Marxists, and anti-constitutional Progressives into our educational, religious, and political institutions (I cover these various groups and movements in my book *Mobocracy*).

By the year 1913, a year I consider to be the beginning of the end of our *Republic* as we knew it and our

Founders designed it, the Federal government began to expand with the establishment of the Federal income tax, the Internal Revenue Service, and the ridiculous politicking over the marginal or progressive tax rates. Woodrow Wilson's progressive government implemented, through the influence of Karl Marx's *Communist Manifesto* and other socialistic-progressive philosophies, a **punitive tax** on income. Our Founders would have considered this an assault on the liberty of personal income, which was one's own sacred property. Over one hundred years ago, the Federal government's IRS began its long-armed encroachment in our lives and pocketbooks, and they have never looked back. Going from 2 percent of the economy in 1912 to 25 percent and growing in 2015, the Federal monster eats away at our economic liberties. Thomas Jefferson tells us that "it is not by the consolidation or concentration of powers, but by their distribution that good government is effected." Progressives like Woodrow Wilson loved the concentration of power in Washington and were able to ratify the Seventeenth Amendment to the Constitution in 1913 where Federal Senators were no longer elected by state legislatures. This amendment became one of the most destructive laws in America as it crippled the very essence of authentic Federalism where sovereign states had a significant say in the composition of the Nations central government's power base. With the creation of the progressive Seventeenth Amendment, State sovereignty diminished, and central government flourished at the expense of the people's sovereignty and liberty.

From the secret creation of the Federal Reserve and the dubious legitimacy of the Sixteenth and Seventeenth Amendments to FDR's New Deal, the size and scope of the Federal government has exploded. Progressives like Wilson and Roosevelt helped create an unelected "Administrative State" where Federal government bureaucrats are destroying our Founders' vision of a limited *Federal republican* government. This oligarchical power structure in our increasingly highly centralized **"D.C. STATE"** has created tens of thousands of rules; regulations and bureaucracies have circumvented and ignored our Constitution while expanding the government and limiting liberty.

Today, we have a bogus narrative that is taught in our government schools that FDR's New Deal saved America during the Great Depression. On the contrary. To paraphrase Hillsdale College history professor Burt Folsom, "FDR's progressive New Deal was an economic legacy that was a raw deal which damaged and changed U.S. political and economic life forever." FDR's "Raw Deal" saw the Federal government double in size as his central government ideas replaced "We the People" with "We the Bigger Government" that controlled more and more of the people's lives, property, and income through a myriad of Federal government programs.

FDR not only used the Great Depression to expand Federal power, he used WWII to justify the explosion of Washington, D.C., over our lives. The so-called temporary Federal Withholding Income Tax of 1943 was to disappear like Karl Marx's ubiquitous State after the War. It never did.

In his 1988 book *Washington Goes to War,* David Brinkley writes very lucidly about the origins of the Federal withholding tax when he states:

> "There began a brutal, bare-knuckled assault on the lives and property and privacy of the American people. The withholding tax poured in more money than Beardsley Ruml (former chairman of R.H. Macy and Co. and of the Federal Reserve Bank of New York) could ever have imagined, partly because government soon learned what automobile and real-estate salesmen already knew – if you talk to the customer about monthly payments, never mentioning the total price, it is much easier to sell a car or a house. In tax collections, the term `take-home pay' entered the language, and soon it was clear the government could take in far more without serious complaint if it deducted the money before the taxpayer ever saw it. If the immense sums being collected had to be handed over in one lump sum, surely there would have been a revolt. The withholding tax allowed government to keep the rates high, [Congress] held on to it, an artesian well spouting cash, computers to count it and disburse it, an automatic, power-driven money machine never seen before and a true wonder of the world. With all this money theirs to spend, congressmen could buy votes and build post offices and roads and bridges and reelect themselves almost interminably. They did."

FDR's 1943 withholding tax was a brilliant ploy to fool the American people into thinking the "Victory Tax" would go away once Hitler and Tojo were defeated. The 1943 withholding tax has become an **eternal Losing TAX** that took the 1913 Federal Income Tax from a "Class Tax" to a "Mass Tax" that still haunts us to this day as politicians and presidents from both parties play with our money for power and proletariat social engineering. They lied to us then, and they are still lying to us today. *Mother, should we trust the government?* History and common sense tells us:

Non, Nei, Nej, Nem, Nai, Nao, Nie, Ne, Ni, Nein, Niet, Lo & NO!

A classic example of a distrustful government operation occurred in February of 1942 during World War II. FDR issued Executive Order 9066 where the Federal government, without due process of constitutional law, evicted 70,000 American citizens of Japanese heritage from their homes and imprisoned them in internment camps. These 70,000 Americans were loyal Patriots, but due to government racism and war paranoia, the Federal government violated their God-given rights and civil liberties. One of those loyal American citizens, Robert Kashiwagi, was stunned as he stated at the time: "As far as I'm concerned, I was born here, and according to the Constitution that I studied in school, that I had the Bill of Rights that should have backed me up. And until the very minute I got on to the evacuation train, I says, 'It can't be'. I says, 'How can they do that to an American citizen?'" Sad but true my fellow American Robert Kashiwagi, many times in life we cannot trust the government as it's propensity is to harm us and not help us.

FDR's corrupt unconstitutional executive action, along with central government Congressional approval and FBI, OMI, and MID spying and surveillance of private citizens' lives, turned out to be a federal fascist act that will live in infamy. I still remember as a kid in the Sixties when I first saw the famous picture of young American children – citizens of African, Chinese, European and Japanese heritage – saying The Pledge of Allegiance in front of the American Flag at Raphael Weill Public School. Within a few months of that pledge, the American-Japanese children were imprisoned in a relocation camp. Another picture that sadden my heart was the 1942 picture of a grocery store owner in Oakland, California, an American citizen of Japanese heritage, who place a huge sign in his store that declared "I AM AN AMERICAN." That American citizen was imprisoned for three years during World War II. Shame on the government, shame on FDR for their tyrannical measures against free American citizens! I have always taught my students that being an American is one word: LIBERTY, or Freedom from government harm. At least many years later under the 1988 Civil Liberties Act that was signed into Law by President Ronald Reagan, the Federal government admitted it's wrong doing and attempted to compensate the citizens they had harmed forty plus years earlier.

Another clever tool to dismantle our limited government *republic* was through a perverted progressive reinterpretation of the so-called General Welfare, Commerce, Necessary and

Proper, and Supremacy *clauses* in the Constitution. With a very broad and liberal "living Constitution" interpretation of our "Rule Book," we saw Uncle Sam grow fatter and fatter, similar to Santa Claus as the Federal government began regulating our lives like never before.

One such story is the story of Roscoe Filburn. Roscoe was an Ohio farmer who maintained a dairy farm selling milk and poultry. In 1940 Roscoe simply wanted to plant twenty-three acres of wheat on his farm during the Great Depression to feed his livestock and make flour for home consumption. Through a ridiculous distortion of the *original intent* and plain language of the Constitution as understood by our Founders, FDR's fascist government created the AAA or the Agricultural Adjustment Act in 1938.

In an attempt to regulate wheat prices, FDR's Big-government AAA demanded that Roscoe could only grow wheat on 11.1 acres and fined him forty-nine cents per bushel over the government limit. The Federal government unconstitutionally declared that Roscoe, an American citizen and a small Ohio farmer who was harvesting wheat on his private property for private consumption and feed for his animals with no personal profit, **violated interstate Commerce!** This is the epitome of absurdity, government arrogance, and tyranny versus life and liberty during FDR's administration.

NEVER did our Founders envision such a profound violation of liberty in the land! Roscoe Filburn rightly felt wronged by Congress and FDR's AAA, since in no way did he logically violate interstate commerce. Filburn argued that the law went way beyond the enumerated powers of Congress and violated his right to simply grow wheat on his property. Additionally, Congress also had no power to regulate wheat that was locally consumed and not sold on the open market in Ohio, let alone beyond the borders of Ohio.

In the infamous *Wickard v. Filburn Case* (Claude R. Wickard was then serving as the Secretary of Agriculture), a unanimous BIG BROTHER Supreme Court ruled in discombobulated and Orwellian language that "though it may not be regarded as commerce, it may still, whatever its nature, be reached by Congress if it exerts a substantial economic effect on interstate commerce."

FDR's AAA stopped everyday, common citizens like Roscoe Filburn and thousands of others from using their property to feed their families and farm animals. This very same Federal government AAA bureaucracy also slaughtered over six million hogs and millions of cattle and demanded that cotton, wheat, and other crops be plowed under at the height of hunger and starvation during the Great Depression. FDR's Big-government Raw Deal experimentation was a disaster for millions of Americans!

Another FDR Big-government Raw Deal program was the NRA, the National Recovery Administration, which acted as the bureaucratic mechanism for the National Industrial Recovery Act of 1933. The NRA was established to improve the economy by regulating codes of "fair" competition. The belief was that government would force the "cartelization" of labor by demanding unions and other industries to set prices to eliminate competition which would theoretically create prosperity and jobs for millions. There were more than five hundred Federal NRA codes and laws that regulated women's corsets, light bulbs, and the cleaning and pressing of men's pants. In her history of the New Deal, Amity Shales declared that the NRA "generated more paper than the entire legislative output of the Federal government since 1789."

Businesses were forced to display the NRA Blue Eagle as a sign of their "cooperation" with the Federal government. In Philadelphia the new NFL football team chose the "Eagle" for their mascot in 1933, as it was reminiscent of FDR's "popular" 1933 Blue Eagle. An admirer of Fascist Benito Mussolini and a man who profoundly influenced FDR's Big-government progressivism, General High "Iron Pants" Johnson headed the NRA and arrogantly declared, "May God have mercy on the man or group of men who attempt to trifle with this bird!"[1]

In 1934 Jacob Maged, aged 49 and a father of four, ran a tailoring and cleansing business in New Jersey, and he dared "to trifle with" FDR's Blue Eagle. FDR's NRA's bureaucrats or "brains that you couldn't trust" knew that THE best price for pressing a man's suit was forty cents throughout the industry. Exercising his liberty as a free citizen to establish his own price in a supposed free market, Maged set his price at thirty-five cents. The long arm of FDR's NRA fined Jacob $100 (approximately $1,800

---

1   George F. Will, "Trifle With the Government? Just Ask Jacob Maceb," *Washington Post*: http://www.washingtonpost.com/wp-dyn/content/article/2010/09/15/AR2010091505090.html (September 16, 2010).

in 2015 dollars) and was sentenced to thirty days in jail. During the trial Maged, who was an immigrant from Poland, thought the punishment was a joke as he lived in America and "these kinds of tyrannical things don't happen in the land of liberty." The sentence was a judicial jest to scare and sober Maged up as to the seriousness of the government's FDR-NRA codes. The judge lectured Maged "on the importance of cooperation as opposed to individualism and disobeying President Roosevelt and General Johnson."[2]

Jacob Maged, whose spirit was broken by the intimidations of the Federal government, removed his thirty-five-cent sign advertisement for pressing suits and replaced it with the ubiquitous Big-government Blue Eagle, an Eagle eerily reminiscent of Germany's National Socialist Eagle. Jacob Maged is a sad example of what happens far too often when an individual citizen exercises his private liberty in the face of a Federal government that arrogantly thinks it knows how to run our lives and restrict our liberties through coercion.

The Nobel Prize winner of Economics Milton Friedman observed: "Pick at random any three letters from the alphabet, put them in any order, and you will have an acronym designating a federal agency we can do without."

"A federal agency we can do without." We could do without many Federal agencies, or we at least need a significant downsizing of what we already have in Washington, D.C., but unfortunately, Milton Friedman with tongue-in-cheek

---

2   Ibid.

is brutally honest when he writes, "Nothing is so permanent as a temporary government program." I'm afraid to say far too many Federal government agencies are here for many generations to come. In his brilliant article *From Administrative State to Constitutional Government*, Joseph Postell writes:

> "Over the past 100 years, our government has been transformed from a limited, constitutional, federal republic to a centralized administrative state that for the most part exists outside the structure of the Constitution and wields nearly unlimited power. This administrative state has been constructed as a result of a massive expansion of the national government's power.

> "When the Founders created our Constitution, they entrusted only limited powers to the national government and specifically enumerated those powers in the Constitution itself. A government that only had to carry out a limited number of functions could do so through the institutions and procedures established by the Constitution.

> "But as the national government expanded and began to focus more and more on every aspect of citizens' lives, the need for a new kind of government—one focused on regulating the numerous activities of citizens rather than on protecting their individual rights—became apparent. In the United States, this new form of government is the

administrative state. In *Democracy in America,* Alexis de Tocqueville warned that under such a government, citizens would become "nothing more than a herd of timid and industrious animals, of which the government is the shepherd.

"As the modern administrative State has grown and metastasized over the past decades, it has taken many forms, to the point of becoming the primary method of politics and policymaking. The myriad agencies and departments that make up this administrative State operate as a "fourth branch" of government that typically combines the powers of the other three and makes policy with little regard for the rights and views of citizens. In terms of actual policy, most of the action is located in administrative agencies and departments, not in the Congress and the President as is commonly thought. Unelected bureaucrats—not elected representatives—are running the show.

"One of the greatest long-term challenges facing the United States is the restoration of limited constitutional government. Central to that objective, and an essential aspect of changing America's course, is the dismantling of the administrative State that so threatens our self-governing republic."

Throughout this little book I have stressed that the people must always watch the "government Shepherd" like a hawk. Unfortunately, many of the people have become "sheeple," as they have succumbed to the enticement of a redistribution welfare state that creates a false security at the expense of liberty. This is not just a Democrat Party creation. Yes, it's true that the progressive Democrat Woodrow Wilson was profoundly guilty of violating the principles of a limited, constitutional *republic* when he helped establish the Federal Reserve, the Federal Progressive Income Tax, the Espionage Act, the Sedition Act, and got us into a needless World War and exploded the Federal bureaucracy like never before. But the progressive Republicans Teddy Roosevelt and Herbert Hoover also expanded the Federal government in huge order as Herbert Hoover, along with a Republican Congress, not only undid the marvelous work of Republican President Calvin Coolidge, but raised the progressive tax rate, passed the job- destroying Smoot Hawley Tariff, and joined with the Federal Reserve in creating the Great Depression.

And let us not forget that the Republican Richard "we-are-all-Keynesians-now" Nixon was responsible for very *un-republican* Big-government actions. Allan Wendt in the *Washington Post* summarizes Nixon well by stating:

> "Nixon's enduring domestic legislation created
> the Environmental Protection Agency, the Clean
> Air and Water Acts, the earned income tax credit,
> Equal Employment Opportunity Act, Endangered
> Species Act and the Occupation Safety and Health
> Administration, among other progressive leg-
> islation. Indeed, in many respects Nixon was a
> demonstrably liberal president."

Yes, Richard Nixon was not a true platform Republican or for that matter a limited-government *republican*. From Wilson's New Federalism, FDR's Raw Deal to LBJ's not-so-Great Society to Nixon's expansion of Federal agencies and Barack Obama's *Transformation Socialism*, many within both major American political parties are guilty of violating the fundamental principle of a limited Federal government as a servant to the people, not a slave master over the people.

Too much government activity and control makes government bloated and bad. A classic *republican* dictum is "the government that governs best governs least" and as Ronald Reagan once said: "government isn't the solution to our problems, government is the problem." We live in a day and age when the media and many people think the more laws and government we have, the more liberty we secure. That is not true.

To understand America's problems and the cultural and political war to destroy our Republic under God, I always want to know what the Elite Media is doing; therefore, I watch the furthest Left, BIG-Media outlet, MSNBC. The other day *Daily Rundown's* Chuck Todd in a sarcastic tone stated, "Is it safe to *declare* the *113th Congress* the least productive on record?" Todd proceeded to lambast the Republicans in Congress as obstructionists, comparing them to the so-called GOP "Do-Nothing 80th Congress" under Harry Truman during the 1947-1949 term.

Sometimes the best thing for Congress to do is **Nothing!** After WWII the Buck-Stops-Here President Truman wanted to explode the Federal government with taxes, spending, and advancing FDR's New Deal through his so-called Fair Deal that desired to "spread the wealth" and expand socialism in America like never before. Those 1947-1949 Republicans believing in their platform, which called for Founding-Father, limited republicanism, refused to go along with Truman's Big-government progressive schemes. Therefore, they did **nothing** as good, limited-government representatives should always do in the face of Big government's propensity to pass more and more laws, legislation, rules, and regulations that rarely, if ever, limit government but almost always expand government and limit liberty.

Since Barack Obama took office, Lefty politicos and talking heads have led the mantra that Republicans are evil obstructionists and not willing to work with Democrats on passing more laws. With one-third of the power, the GOP House has legally, constitutionally, and legitimately slowed down the passing of various laws that they deemed unconstitutional or were designed to advance Democrat-Socialism.

The bottom line is: There IS a profound difference between their ideological platforms. Democrats call for socialism and the expansion of Federal government power in Washington, D.C., while Republicans call for authentic, limited government based on the republicanism of our Founders.

Hold on Tea Partiers and libertarians! Don't nuts on me! Yes, I know many Republicans within the establishment don't practice their platform and aren't guided by those principles, but some in the Republican Party do and are at least fighting to slow down the Democrat Big Brother Machine. If only all of our Republican representatives acted and voted by their platform like the Democrats do, we'd be much better off.

Our Founding Fathers had principles that were always suspect of government's good intentions through an inordinate amount of legislation, especially through a Central government at the Federal level. They knew that the great Roman Statesman Tacitus warned that "the more numerous the laws, the more corrupt the state." This dictum guided our Founders in designing a *Republic* that while profoundly believing in the Rule of Law, believed we were to have a few, limited laws to protect freedom, but not too many laws to harm life and destroy liberty.

This is why *republicans* like Thomas Jefferson, George Mason, Patrick Henry, and Samuel Adams wrote and lectured over and over again against excessive Central government legislation that would diminish liberty. The Father of our Constitution, James Madison, warned us that, "It will be of little avail to the people that the laws are made by men of their own choice if the laws be so voluminous that they cannot be read, or so incoherent that they cannot be understood."

Thomas Jefferson taught us that the US Constitution gave Congress the power to criminally punish "treason, counterfeiting the securities and current coin of the United States, piracies, and felonies committed on the high seas, and offenses against the law of nations, and no other crimes whatever." Today the Federal criminal code has listed over 4,450 criminal laws and growing.

The Federal Registry of over 75,000 pages records all of the Federal government regulations and imposes thousands of rules on businesses in America today. The Federal tax code of 1913 was 400 pages; today it approaches 75,000 pages with 700 forms and is administered by over 90,000 bureaucrats with thousands of rules and regulations on hard working American citizens and costs taxpayers well over eleven billion dollars yearly. If you read 750 pages of the US Federal Code a week, it would take 19 years to complete. That is just at the Federal level. Imagine adding the unfortunate growing amount of State legislation to that list.

In 2008 presidential candidate Barack Obama promised to make his administration and the Federal government the most transparent in history. What a joke! According to an August 5, 2014, *USA Today* article on the latest report into government transparency:

> *A government website intended to make federal spending more transparent was missing at least $619 billion from 302 federal programs, a government audit has found.*
> *And the data that does exist is wildly inaccurate, according to the Government Accountability Office, which looked at 2012 spending data. Only 2% to 7% of spending data on* USASpending.gov *is "fully consistent with agencies' records."*

The report comes as the Obama administration begins to implement the Digital Accountability and Transparency Act, which Congress passed last year to expand the amount of federal spending data available to the public. The report said the Office of Management and Budget needed to exercise greater oversight of federal agencies reporting spending data. "Until these weaknesses are addressed, any effort to use the data will be hampered by uncertainties about accuracy," the report said.

OMB spokesman Jamal Brown said the administration is already working to improve the data following the passage of the DATA Act last year. "OMB is committed to federal spending transparency and working with agencies to improve the completeness and accuracy of data submissions," he said in a statement.

The administration is also transferring responsibility for the website from the General Services Administration to the Bureau of the Fiscal Service in the Department of the Treasury.

Ronald Reagan brilliantly declared in his classic 1964 *Time for Choosing* speech:

"No government ever voluntarily reduces itself in size. So governments programs, once launched, never disappear. Actually, a government bureau is the nearest thing to eternal life we'll ever see on this earth."

As Federal government officials from the President of the United States to Federal Bureaus and Department

administrators promise us transparency and accountability, we the people are lied to over and over again as
"government grows and liberty decreases."

And as covered earlier, don't forget that the "Fourth
Branch" of progressive government, **The Un-Elected
Administrative-Bureaucratic State,** is working in tandem
with an unconstitutional Federal government growing
government like never before! Can this government mad-
ness ever be stopped?

Any government big enough through voluminous laws
to theoretically give you everything you want is big enough
to destroy your God-given life and liberties. If my study
of history has taught me anything, it is that almost all bad
government derives from Big government, which was created by too many laws that made it BIG in the first place.
As government laws grow, our liberties die. The *republican*
statesman Thomas Jefferson wisely stated, "A wise and
frugal government which shall restrain men from injuring one another, which shall leave them otherwise free to
regulate their own pursuits of industry and improvement,
and shall not take from the mouth of labor the bread it has
earned. This is the sum of good government."

The sum of good government is not more rules and
regulations or more laws and legislation. The sum of good
government is not only restraining men from hurting each
other, but it is retraining itself from injuring the people! To
achieve such restraint today, it would be wise and prudent
to simply live by the basic laws of our Constitution as originally understood and to apply God's Ten Commandments

to our lives. In doing so, we would once again discover the beauty of our *Republic under God* and the liberty a limited Constitutional government secures.

So while the Lefty-Elite Media pundits might pontificate and lambast the GOP and the so-called do-nothing Congress, I declare that in the spirit of authentic *republicanism* of 1776, "the government that governs best governs least." Go home Congress, and leave us alone Washington, D.C.!

Suggested Reading:

Theodore and Woodrow by Andrew P. Napolitano

New Deal or Raw Deal? by Burton Folsom, Jr.

Who Killed the Constitution? by Thomas E. Woods and Kevin Gutzman

Jake at Michigan Conservative-GOP Conference speaking on Statism

CHAPTER 7

CONCLUSION – KEEPING OUR AMERICAN REPUBLIC

We are five days away from fundamentally trans-forming the United States of America.

—Barack Obama, October 30, 2008

M y 2011 book *Mobocracy* covers in detail my concern over the anti-Constitutional, anti-*Republic* direction Barack Hussein Obama is taking America. As early as 2007, I was writing and speaking out on the disastrous effect an Obama presidency would have on our *Republic*. Obama and his Democrat cohorts have accelerated the growth of government like no president in our history since Franklin Delano Roosevelt. Monica Crowley states it brilliantly when she writes:

"I recalled how Barack Obama spoke in 2008 about the 'fundamental transformation of the nation.' After five years of his presidency, we see the enormous success he's had in achieving it. The objective was always to move America away from a nation built on individual liberty and economic freedom and toward a government welfare and dependency state. Socialism, communism, statism, leftism – in the end it doesn't matter what you call it, because what matters is what's being carried out – and its consequences. Radical wealth redistribution, class warfare, socialized medicine, the atomization of American society, divisive identity politics, the war on success, the loss of our Triple-A credit rating, the retrenchment of U.S. power abroad, the gutting of our military, the erosion of our international credibility.

"It's all being done deliberately by Obama and the Left in order to 'fundamentally transform' this country into just another crippled dependency state. After five years of evidence, people are still wondering aloud why Obama doesn't negotiate, why he doesn't compromise, why he doesn't handle things the way, say, Bill Clinton did.

"Wake the BLEEP up! Unlike Clinton, who was a pragmatist, Obama is a pure ideologue. Why do you think he hasn't negotiated with Republicans? (A) Because he doesn't really have to, given that the Left in Congress and the media protect and advance his interests at every turn and because the GOP is so spineless, and (B) Because he's a total ideologue who will never give anything on his way to 'fundamentally transforming the nation.'"

Barack Obama is a total ideologue! He is DRIVEN by

progressive, socialistic, left wing BIG-GOVERNMENT **ideas** that have been with him since his high school years. This is cogently covered in Paul Kengor's book *THE COMMUNIST: Frank Marshall Davis: The Untold Story of Barack Obama's Mentor* and Stanley Kurtz's *RADICAL-IN-CHIEF: Barack Obama and the Untold Story of American Socialism.* Barack Obama's *anti-republican* ideas are why I have stressed throughout this book the *"republican"* **ideological** origins of America. Those **ideas** are KEY and essential in understanding our Constitutional *Federal Republic under God* where government is limited and liberty is enhanced. Barack Obama's progressive, Big-government worldview was developed early in his life from his socialist mother Stanley Ann Dunham and communist father Barack Obama, Sr., to his high school mentor, the famous communist Frank Marshall Davis and his Progressive, Left Wing education at Columbia and Harvard where he learned Marxist Critical Theory and adhered to the "Progressive" interpretation of American history that stresses class warfare, social justice, and economic equality, while downplaying or ignoring the profound impact *whig-republican* ideas had on our Founders.

The brilliant Harvard Professor of Early American History, Bernard Bailyn, in his equally brilliant book *The Ideological Origins of The American Revolution*, challenges the Progressive view that *whig* and *republican* rhetoric was of little value when compared to an economic and social interpretation of our Republic's origin. Bailyn rightfully argues that the *whig-republican* Revolutionary rhetoric of freedom, liberty, and limited government was not simply propagandistic verbiage but was central to their worldview and played a key role in their passionate desire to create a free and independent *Republic*. When Obama was at Harvard, he unfortunately never learned proper American Revolution history as taught by the brilliant Bernard Bailyn, but he did learn all the Left Wing progressive claptrap and poppycock that has been very popular at Ivy League Schools since the Sixties.

This attempt at transforming our Federal Republic is not new. James Madison recognized it in 1798 when he and Thomas Jefferson penned the Kentucky and Virginia Resolutions. Madison wrote in the Virginia Resolutions protesting President John Adams' Alien and Sedition Acts that Adams was attempting "to transform the present republican system of the United States into an absolute, or at best, a mixed monarchy."

The biased Democrat historian Arthur Schlesinger, a "JFK-RFK-ophile," labeled Richard Nixon the "Imperial President." We have been fighting the tendency of our Executives to act imperialistic since John Adams, and now with Barack Obama the "Imperial Presidency" has exploded!

Here are a few examples of the lies, deception, and unconstitutional actions of the Obama administration since January 20, 2009, from Tim Brown's *FrontPage Magazine* article *252 Examples of Obama's Lies, Law-breaking & Corruption:*

Carried out military interventionism in Libya without Congressional approval

Gave a no-bid contract to Halliburton – just like Bush did

Has an administration full of lobbyists, after promising he wouldn't have any

Lied about letting people keep their health insurance

Lied about putting health care negotiations on C-SPAN

Has close ties to Wall St., but pretends to support Occupy Wall Street

Broke his promise to close Guantanamo Bay

Supported the $700 billion TARP corporate-welfare bailout just like Bush

Nominated a six-time tax cheater to head the government agency that enforces the tax laws

Gave tax dollars to AIG executives and then pretended to be outraged about it

Increased the national debt more in one term than Bush did in two

Agrees with Bush's support of unconstitutional, indefinite detention of U.S. citizens without filing any charges

Agrees with Bush's support of unconstitutional, warrantless wiretapping

Avoided prosecution of Wall Street criminals

Had four U.S. citizens killed without judicial process

Ordered private company to fire 1,000 employees

Stole money from retired teachers and police officers

Supported release of convicted mass murderer

Put thousands of guns into the hands of criminals in Operation Fast and Furious

Fired Inspector General for discovering that Obama's friend had embezzled government funds

Lied about the cost of Obamacare

Gave tax dollars to campaign contributors and lobbyists, and falsely claimed the money was for "green energy"

Falsely claimed to believe in public education

Had armed SWAT agents raid a law-abiding guitar factory because a Republican owned it
Rewarded his fundraisers by giving them federal jobs

Ignored constitutional requirements for appointees

Gave tax dollars to corrupt private contractors

Allowed Political profiling by the IRS

Expansion of the employer mandate penalty through IRS regulation

Exemption of Congress from Obamacare

There are many, many more examples of Obama administration's corruption, deception, and obfuscation to the lying, spying, and cover-ups within the DOJ, IRS, NSA, EPA, HSA, DOT, DHS, VA and many more. It is sadly and profoundly obvious: Mother, **we cannot trust the government!**

I have had the honor of working with the brilliant lawyer, author and TV commentator Ben Shapiro at *Young America's Foundation Reagan Ranch Center* in Santa Barbara, California. Ben's new book, *The People vs. Barack Obama*, is a stinging indictment on the unconstitutional and lawless activity of the Obama administration. Here is the Amazon.com summary of his seminal work:

"From the DOJ to the NSA, from the EPA to the Department of Health and Human Services, Barack Obama's administration has become a labyrinth of corruption and overreach touching every aspect of Americans' lives. *The People vs. Barack Obama* strips away the soft media picture of the Obama administration to reveal a regime motivated by pure, unbridled power and details how each scandal has led to dozens of instances of as-yet-unprosecuted counts of espionage, involuntary manslaughter, violation of internal revenue laws, bribery, and obstruction of justice.

"The story of the Obama administration is a story
of abuse, corruption, and venality on the broadest
scale ever to spring from the office of the presidency.
President Obama may be the culmination of a century of government growth, but more important, he
is the apotheosis of the imperial presidency. Obama
chooses when to enforce immigration laws, delays
his own Obamacare proposals when it is politically
convenient to do so, micromanages the economy,
attacks the Supreme Court, Congress, and the sovereign states. And he proclaims that he alone is the
voice of the people while encroaching on their rights.
In *The People vs. Barack Obama*, Ben Shapiro brings
Obama into the people's court and addresses each of
his abuses of power."

In *The People vs. Barack Obama* Shapiro writes,
"Consolidated government means consolidated power,
consolidated power mean consolidated corruption." Earlier
he had stated, "The Obama administration has become
a full-fledged criminal enterprise. Riddled up and down
with executive branch appointees engaged in high crimes
and misdemeanors."

In his article "*The People vs. Barack Obama*" in *Frontpage
Magazine*, Daniel Greenfield states:

"There can be no plausible expectation that
Attorney General Eric Holder will investigate
Obama. Not when Holder is corrupt. As corrupt
confederates in crime, Obama protects Holder and
Holder protects Obama. Likewise, Obama Inc. is

composed of such self-serving mutual pacts forming a system of power that makes up its own laws while refusing to be accountable to the law."

Our Republic's 1789 system of checks and balances and respect for the rule of law has in many ways been done away with. The Obama political machine advances a common ideological goal and purpose: **to undo the work of America's Founders.** One of the major ways they are undoing the work of our Founders and transforming America is the Obama push for immigration "reform" that will grant amnesty to tens of millions of illegals creating a new dependency class that will vote permanently Democratic, thus changing the political demographics of many states in America, especially Texas.

As goes Texas, so goes America! In his book *Fed Up! Our Fight to Save America from Washington*, Texas Governor Rick Perry writes, "One of Washington's greatest failures has been its unwillingness to secure our nation's border … Our broken borders put lives at risk. They make a mockery of the rule of law … The current administration willfully refuses to enforce the laws on the books … The federal government fails us in every facet of its immigration policy."

Texas Governor Perry wrote those words in 2010, when Obama had been in office for over a year. Now, five years later, the illegal immigration border situation has exploded into an unmitigated disaster, causing Governor Perry to send in the National Guard to do the job Obama refuses to do. Obama and the Democrats know exactly what they're doing. They are crunching the illegal immigrant numbers, and they know the numbers and time are on their side.

Texas has America's second largest number of electoral votes at 38, and California has long ago stopped being a Reagan Red State, as their 55 votes are forever Democrat Blue. With New York's Blue 29 and Florida's Blue 29, a Texas 38 Blue could be disastrous for Republicans and America. Texas has been a solid Red Republican State for years and is an excellent example of a successful State government fighting Federal government mandates and tyranny. Due to the onslaught of illegal immigrants, Texas is at a disconcerting rate of Democrat demographics that, if not stopped, will change Texas from Republican Red to Democrat Blue. It isn't there yet, but if Texas goes the "Blue path of California," Democrats will dominate the Electrical College for the next hundred years and have *carte blanche* power to fulfill their transformative progressive vision of a new un-*republican* America.

Obama and the Democrat Big-government machinery know exactly what they are doing as they collude with the illegal immigration onslaught in America. This partnership is contributing significantly to the transformation and slow death of our *Republic under God*. Yes, this death started way before Barack Obama's ascendance to his "Presidential Throne," but Obama's executive lawlessness has accelerated this progressive process and unless the American people wake up and fight for liberty, freedom will continue to descend into the depths way beyond Obama's Reign.

From Aaron Klein's *RED ARMY: The Radical Network*

That Must Be Defeated To Save America to Trevor Loudon's *THE ENEMIES WITHIN: Communists, Socialists and Progressives In The U.S. Congress*, there is a preponderance of evidence that the tide of a perfect storm is on the horizon that could produce a tidal wave of tyrannical government we have not seen in America since 1775. I hope and pray I am wrong.

In my fight to keep our American Republic, I have been traveling across our great land from California to Pennsylvania, meeting thousands of dedicated Patriots who are in the trenches battling tyranny. They give me hope. In Michigan, people like Marco and Sharon Lollio whom I met while speaking at a Michigan Conservative conference. The Lollios are hard-working Christians, small business owners who after seeing the despotic direction of our Nation under Barack Obama have become involved in politics. They call themselves "platform Republicans" and are movers and shakers in Michigan, working to awaken Americans to the fact that our Republic is in danger. Their son Tony is a writer and a dedicated Patriot who has been working with Christian conservatives, Republicans, and Libertarians in the common cause for Life and Liberty. Tony's mother Sharon shared with me a piece he wrote a few years ago, and I am honored to share it with you in my book. Here are Tony Lollio's words of encouragement for those who in the spirit of the Tea Party movement want to keep our Republic:

> *Stay on track, Tea Party; you're taking flak because you're over the target. Powerful people have arrayed themselves*

against you, because you refused to just go away. You come from every walk of life; but you stand here together and speak with one voice – one very powerful voice that seems to be echoing through the nooks and crannies of our great country. You believe that this nation was founded on certain principles that are timeless, and that our Founding Fathers provided us a tangible road map to the trials that our country would encounter; yet you feel as though a bloated, reeling out of control government has decided to throw that road map out, and you have something to say about it.

Stay on track, Tea Party; you've educated and informed yourselves. You've worn out your pocket Constitutions with highlighters and folded corners; and in doing so, you've equipped yourselves with the knowledge required to begin beating back tyranny and despotism. You find truth somewhere in all the confusion.

Thomas Paine wrote in 1791:

"Freedom had been hunted around the globe, reason was considered as rebellion; and the slavery of fear had men afraid to think. But such is the irresistible nature of truth, that all it asks, and all it wants, is the liberty of appearing."

I believe truth is beginning to appear. I believe eyes are opening. I believe a giant is awakening. I believe that real "hope and change" starts with an informed citizenry. I believe that real "recovery" begins when responsible individuals take charge of their own destinies and demand that their elected government stay out of their way while they do so. The time for action is right now, and you are taking action; for that, some will seek to destroy you.

Stay on track, Tea Party; now is not the time to be distracted by slander and cheap shot tactics. You've faced it before; you've weathered the storm of Community organizers, of the professional and sometimes taxpayer-funded organizations arrayed against you, and you refuse to go away. You refuse to not be heard. You refuse to believe a lie being force fed to you by biased media outlets, crooked bureaucracies, and by liberal professors and elitists who seek to fundamentally change America in the name of social justice, as though it hadn't already been tried so many times before.

Stay on track, Tea Party; because the future of this country demands the vigilance of its citizens. A group of Leftist Ideologues has been snatching away liberty from the people at an astonishing rate of speed. In his farewell address in 1796, George Washington speaks of, "Potent engines by which cunning, ambitious, and unprincipled men will be enabled to subvert the power of the people and to usurp for themselves the reigns of government, destroying afterwards the very engines which have lifted them to their unjust dominion." Do you believe these forces are at work right now in America?

Stay on track, Tea Party: Though they will call you Rednecks, Racists, bigots, and tea baggers. Remember that the names they call you are derogatory slurs and

*that you are being profiled; and every time they hurl an
insult at you, they expose their own hypocrisy by doing
the very thing they claim to stand against. They will look
for every opportunity to discourage and demoralize you,
because it is you that stands between them and their ultimate goal. You are very sure to face an entrenched and
determined foe; large amounts of money have and will be
spent on lies and smear campaigns meant to undermine
the credibility of your cause and render you ineffective.
Take care to hold yourselves to a higher standard, to not
be baited or distracted and so divided. Keep your eyes
steady on the prize, which in our Republic is the ballot
box.*

*Stay on track, Tea Party; because a majority of
Americans still love this country as much as you do, and
in true grassroots movements all over America, those
people are finally finding an advocate and a voice. A
voice that says, 'We are flat out tired of wasteful government spending. We are sick of borrowing money to
fund broken and fiscally irresponsible programs. We're
done with deficits. We are finished apologizing to other
countries for our greatness. We have a right to protect
ourselves, our families, and our borders. We've had
enough of big, obnoxious, omniscient government trying to control what doctors we see, what cars we drive,
how we invest our money, the foods we eat, the air we
breathe. We are sick of the type of entitlement mentality
that causes men to become slaves to whatever party cuts
them the biggest check. Slavery is the opposite of freedom.*

We believe Washington should be setting the free market free, so instead of welfare and unemployment checks, folks could get paychecks.

Stay on track, Tea Party. Stay vigilant. Remember that Americans are exceptional, because while we believe that all people on earth were created equal, we understand that the Founding Fathers provided us with a set of documents that has allowed us to ascend over the past two and a half centuries. Defend those documents; they lay out a system of government based on the consent of the governed, which is a treasure that I hope my children will enjoy, and their children will enjoy, and so on for another two and a half centuries.

When I read Tony's words out loud with Tony's parents in the room, I could see how proud they were of his dedication to keeping our Republic, and I could see the pain of two parents knowing that their son was suffering from Lou Gehrig's disease and could no longer write such beautiful words defending life and liberty.

I have the honor of speaking on the life of President Ronald Reagan for Young America's Foundation at the Reagan Ranch Center in Santa Barbara, California. I am inspired and given hope when I meet young Americans for freedom and their parents from across America. When I meet Dylan Rhodehamel and his mother Jo and I see the patriotic passion they have for keeping our Republic as they are working hard in Tucson and Flagstaff, Arizona educating Americans on our Federal Republic, I am encouraged.

Then there's the Donnelly family from California. In 2013 I met high school student Daniel Donnelly at the Reagan Ranch Center, and he said he was inspired to continue the fight for our Republic after hearing me speak on President Reagan and insisted I meet his father Tim. The moment I met Tim I knew he and his family were dynamos for liberty! Tim is a Christian conservative and Assemblymen in Sacramento working hard for the people of California. Tim spent two years running for governor of California and amazingly going up against both the Democrat and Republican establishment, Tim finished third. While he may have lost the race, he has won the hearts of millions of Californians and Americans who admire his tenacious dedication to keeping our Republic. Here is his story in his own words:

> *I am Assemblyman Tim Donnelly. I spent exactly four years in politics, and in that time shook the GOP establishment to its core, ran for Governor on a shoestring budget, and almost won the nomination.*

> *When I was first elected to office in 2010, I thought I knew how government worked, or more accurately, didn't. Little did I know that I was about to get a front-row seat to the power struggle between the people and the politicians who pretend to represent them. I won an election that no one expected me to win by a single vote per precinct. What I discovered by walking door-to-door was that most people feel the government doesn't care what they think and doesn't listen to them. They didn't*

need a poll to tell them that – even though poll after poll confirmed that almost 80% of the people feel they have no representation. In spite of raising almost no money, only $15,000 – which may have set a record for the least spent at that time – I was able to harness the votes of 80% of the people simply because I listened to them and gave voice to their deepest concerns.

The first day I drove up to the Capitol, I was nervous they wouldn't let me in. To make matters worse, I had left my wallet back at the hotel. As we drove up to the gate, they asked my name through a speaker. Once given, there was a pause, then the gate lifted, and we drove into the basement of the Capitol. As we drove through, I turned to my friends and said, "They just let the wrong guy in the building."

I'm not sure what I expected, but the reality was much different. Everyone was so accommodating and so nice that it was unnatural. That's when I realized that there were hundreds of people all who make a living off making you feel important. Their entire purpose was to seduce each and every one of us, so that we would be manageable. They convinced the majority of the members that it's all about relationships and that "institutional knowledge" rested with the lobbyists, who refer to themselves as the Third House.

Two things happened early on that made a dramatic impact on me.

Shredder: Getting the word outside the building

One of the first things I learned in Sacramento was that if you want to be relevant, you need to stand out. I learned a hard lesson that first month. The California Constitution states that the Governor must present a balanced budget by January 15th. Our office waited for the budget. It didn't come until late in the afternoon. We were first in line to get a copy. We each took a section of the budget and attempted to analyze it, working feverishly to make heads or tails of it. After an hour or so, we were able to begin writing a press release. I noticed that my email was full of press releases from my colleagues. They had professional staff who wrote the releases before the budget even came out. By the time I pressed "send" on our press release, every one of them was three drinks in. It was just before 8:00 pm.

The next day I was furious. Everyone else had coverage except our office. I felt like I had let down all the people who had sent me to Sacramento. My job was to be their voice, and that only counts if it gets heard. Writing a press release no one ever published was the best mistake I could have made at this early stage.

As I was about to eat lunch, I asked my scheduler to bring my copy of the budget into my office. She set it down on my desk while I was on the phone, and I couldn't help notice how fat the budget was next to my can of Diet Coke. I told her to contact the media office,

*the one that was so busy the day before. Today, they'd be
free for sure.*

*When the caucus media crew showed up, I put them to
work immediately. We worked without a script.*

*I stood behind my desk in a nice suit and tie, and said,
"Hi, I'm Assemblyman Tim Donnelly, and I just received
a copy of Governor Jerry Brown's budget. Look at it." I
held it up.*

*"It's almost as tall as my can of Diet Coke. This is Jerry
Brown's budget, and it needs to go on a diet." As I said
that, I had inadvertently used my middle finger to hold
up the budget. We didn't notice that until we had already
released the video. "Do we really need to spend $652 mil-
lion on a job-killing bureaucracy called CARB?"*

*Then as I tore the entire CARB portion out of the budget,
I said, "We need to make job-killing agencies like CARB
an endangered species in California instead of jobs and
businesses."*

*"Then I looked into the camera and smiled, "Don't worry,
CARB! We'll recycle."*

*Then I crammed the entire sheaf of papers that I had
torn out of the budget book into a shredder labeled
'Government Waste' with an arrow pointing down.*

*The video was some six minutes long, but those first two
minutes were all most people saw.*

I was in state-mandated, sexual-harassment training

when the video hit the press. We emailed out our video to our entire press list and all the constituents who had signed up for legislative updates.

I received an email from Michele Kane, our Caucus media contact, at about 3:00 pm. By 3:15, it hit every newspaper in the state, when the Sacramento Bee put out what's called a Capitol Alert. The next day I was invited to come on radio with the two most influential radio hosts in the state, and they gave me forty-two minutes on air, exposing the way politics really works. That taught me one simple rule; if the media doesn't broadcast it beyond this building, it didn't happen.

How it Works (Raw Power)

In the course of my time serving in the California State Assembly, I discovered that the state of our Republic was far worse than I imagined. Elected as a very conservative, "tea party" type, I immediately became a target from all sides. One thing became clear; once elected, there are no longer any Republicans or Democrats; the politicians meld into one "political power class." They will unite to crush any threat to their cushy lifestyle. Anyone who is serious about reforming government is immediately targeted.

Our first battle on the floor was the Governor's budget. He wanted to raise taxes, and I'd sworn a blood oath to kill his tax increase. As the votes went up on a pre-cursor bill that was part of the package, I worked the floor to protect our members from being pressured into putting up their votes. It was amazing to observe the brutal business of politics in action.

The speaker of the house, John Perez − a massive figure whose reputation was as imposing as his stature − came over and leaned on my desk to woo the vote of an Orange County Assemblyman, Alan Mansour, seated in front of me.

"What do you want, Alan? You want pension reform … done" He snapped his fingers.

Alan asked him, "What about this money we spend on illegals? Can't we do something about that?"

"Sure. You name it. It's yours. You want your name in lights on a reform bill? I can make that happen." The speaker was so intense, that I don't think he noticed me until I interrupted.

"Wait a minute, Alan … did you know that the Higher Ed committee just passed the California Dream Act to spend hundreds of millions on free tuition for illegals?"

The speaker turned to me and said, "Shut up. No one asked your opinion."

I glared at him, my heart pounding. "Well, if you didn't want my opinion, you shouldn't have held your meeting at my desk."

With that, the Speaker leaped to his feet and said, "Close the roll," which would have ended any chance for the bill he was trying to pass. If there were any integrity in those in power, they would have followed his order, but they knew he'd made a mistake. That day was eye-opening. The GOP which held together for the first and only time I was there, savored that one small victory on July 1, 2011, when the Governor's tax increase extension died.

Taking a stand

After that victory, the Democrats worked overtime to bring issues to the forefront that would divide the Republicans. One of the most radioactive issues was the California Dream Act. On October 8, Governor Jerry Brown signed into law a bill that would give any student who is in the country illegally and attends a California High School for three years, free college tuition. The reaction from the public was dramatic. Since I was on record speaking out and building opposition against the measure and had promised to attempt to overturn it by referendum, I began receiving hundreds of emails on my campaign email as soon as news broke on a sleepy fall Saturday.

On Monday October 10, when I announced on the John and Ken show that I had filed a referendum, our newly uploaded website exploded with contacts. Ten thousand signed up to help repeal the Dream Act in the first twenty-four hours. By the end of the week, that had doubled. We polled our responses and found out some interesting statistics: Almost 35% of those helping repeal the Dream Act were Hispanic, and close to 25% were hardcore liberal Democrats, but the most vocal support came from immigrants themselves who had gone through the byzantine maze that is our legal immigration process. After traveling the state and working relentlessly during the recess (time I should have been spending time with my family), our all-volunteer effort fell short. We gathered over 450,000 signatures, but needed 505,000 valid ones to qualify. That means we needed to gather a minimum of 700,000 as many of them would be deemed invalid.

That effort to repeal a bill that granted those in the country illegally free tuition that we do not even offer to those serving in our armed forces was immensely popular among the people, but the GOP establishment showed their true colors about two days before the deadline to submit the signatures.

On January 4, 2012, I was exhausted. I had traveled the state and worked through the Thanksgiving and Christmas Holidays relentlessly in pursuit of signatures. We had thrown together a ramshackle, all-volunteer organization and proceeded to hold signature-gatherings all over the state. California is the largest and the most populous in the union. That made the effort required monumental. To compound matters, at some of our signature-gathering tables, organized protestors of the Chicano Movement intimidated our mostly female volunteers. In response, we had to rally a sufficient number of strong young men to protect them from violence. Death threats were a daily reality.

*On January 1, I thought I was going to the Rose Bowl
with my son, David. Instead, the game was held on
Monday January 2. As a result of getting death threats
including a very serious in person altercation, I decided
to carry my .45 mm with me as I was doing things
around the house. When my wife arrived home, I threw
it into my briefcase temporarily, which was on the work-
bench in my gun room. I never moved it back into my
gun safe. The next day I was at the Rose Bowl all day,
and the day after that I spent at a friend's home. On
January 4, I had to report to Sacramento for work. I
didn't remember that I'd left my gun in bag until I was
going through security. By then it was too late. That incident made breaking national news. In California, it was
front page news for weeks, thanks to the political establishment. The elite power brokers in both parties tried to
influence the DA to charge me with a felony, which would
have ended my political career. Instead, it backfired on
them because I went out to the people and told them the
truth. That incident gave me statewide name ID over
night.*

*During my 2012 reelection campaign, I discovered that
when the people are with you and you are under attack,
it is the most powerful connection of all. The California
GOP had recruited a moderate mayor to challenge me in
2012. In spite of a war chest of over half a million dollars, and another half a million spent attacking me by
unions and GOP establishment shills, I won re-election
in a landslide. In a three man race, where Republican*

registrations are only 43%, I got 52% of the vote, the Democrat got 30%, and the moderate got a mere 19%. In spite of how conservative I am, I pulled Democrat votes. That taught me that if you stand your ground and you level with the people, they will have your back.

As a result of these experiences and countless people asking me to run, I started exploring a bid for the 2014 California Governor's race. For two years, I traveled the state, met tens of thousands of people in person, and galvanized an army of ordinary Americans into dedicated Patriots. In poll after poll after poll, I was crushing the GOP competition, right up to the last few days. But in the end, they expended almost $4.5 million to my $750,000, and in spite of receiving almost 650,000 votes, I came in third behind the GOP establishment candidate. Their pick – an openly pro-choice, pro-gay marriage, pro-amnesty, pro-common core, and virulently anti-second amendment, Goldman-Sachs banker was, in fact, the guy who ran TARP, bailing out the bankers and billionaires – that's who received the backing of GOP heavyweights like Mitt Romney, Jeb Bush, Chris Christie, Condi Rice, Pete Wilson, and Darrel Issa. As we've seen happening all over the country, every time the GOP establishment flexes its money, the people lose.

The simple truth is that anyone who wishes to enter the battle to save our Republic needs to understand that the GOP establishment will soon become the greatest threat to their success. Only after conquering the evil within

our own ranks can we take the battle to the enemies of
freedom.

Back here in Wisconsin there are far too many Patriots
to mention in this small book but I have to include my
friend Michael Schraa, a Christian and small business
man who dared to put a sign in his Leon's Custard shop
supporting Republican Scott Walker for Governor. He was
attacked and boycotted by the local Democrat teachers
union. Unintimidated, Mike stood his ground and helped
Scott Walker become governor of Wisconsin and is now
a dedicated Assemblyman for us in Madison, Wisconsin,
advancing Conservative and republican values. As I'm
writing this, hundreds of citizens come to mind who are
working tirelessly at keeping our American Republic; I
am frustrated that I can't mention them all!

Last but not least is Steven Gillespie who just recently
lost in his attempt for an Assembly seat in Madison,
Wisconsin. Steven serves with me on the board of 1776
American Action and is the Wisconsin State Director for
I Am American, a national organization leading the fight
for a State-led federal Balanced Budget amendment. Here
are a few pages on Steven's viewpoints on how we should
fight to keep our American Republic:

> *There is a dysfunctional relationship today between our*
> *fifty States and Washington, D.C. Our States began as*
> *the "Parents" in a relationship that gave birth to their*
> *"Child," our Federal Government. But somewhere along*
> *the way, the parents gave the child an unlimited credit*
> *card and the ability to sneak its way into our back pocket*

through a confusing tax policy to extract more than we know without us giving any real informed consent.

P. J. O'Rourke has said, "Giving money and power to government is like giving whisky and car keys to teenage boys."

We have a life and death power struggle today with an unruly child, our Federal Government, and it is over control of our money. We have to stop the Feds from spending more than they have and from reaching into our back pocket without permission. Our states need to reassert themselves to take back control, and our Founding Fathers in their wisdom have left the States with the power to make that happen.

That power was given in Article V of our US Constitution, which allows the States equal power to propose amendments. It says:

"The Congress, whenever two thirds of both houses shall deem it necessary, shall propose amendments to this Constitution, or, on the application of the legislatures of two thirds of the several states, shall call a convention for proposing amendments, which, in either case, shall be valid to all intents and purposes, as part of this Constitution, when ratified by the legislatures of three fourths of the several states, or by conventions in three fourths thereof, as the one or the other mode of ratification may be proposed by the Congress;"

Vital action proposing 2 key Amendments is needed today.

Our 18 trillion dollar national debt has brought us to the cusp of national bankruptcy and threatens the survival of our Republic. We are on the verge of economic collapse, where we could see bread lines worse than the Great Depression.

Congress has failed to pass a Balanced Budget Amendment (BBA) for the last 30 years. They are farther from action today than ever. Our States must act where Congress has failed. We need 34 States to file Resolutions with Congress calling for a Convention to propose a Balanced Budget Amendment. Already 24 have done so. Wisconsin, my home-state, is close to joining the effort. In the spring of 2014, we were just 2 votes away from passage.

In the 1980s, President Ronald Reagan came close to passing a Balanced Budget Amendment through Congress. When that failed, he called on the States to act. The 2012 Congressional Report to Congress on the History of the Article V Process reports that Walter Mondale launched a whisper-campaign to counter Reagan's effort. It alleged a Convention of States would run-away and destroy the Constitution by delegates proposing unexpected and radical amendments. The subterfuge slowed passage in the last few states. Congress then passed the Gramm-Rudman-Hollings Deficit Reduction Act that many hoped would rein-in the deficit, and the push for a BBA went to the sidelines. But Patriots are again fanning the flame for a State-led BBA, including conservatives like Senator Rand Paul as well as Mark Levin, Rush Limbaugh, Sean Hannity, and Herman Cain. Their opponents are liberals who enjoy the power they get from using borrowed money to buy votes by expanding Federal programs. Wisconsin's Resolution was sponsored by sixty-five Republicans and 0 Democrats. Opponents can't just say they want to keep spending like drunken sailors. Like Mondale in the 1980s, they repeat the mantra of fearing a "runaway" Convention as the reason for their opposition.

They allege the Constitutional Convention of 1787 "ran-away" because delegates went beyond Congress's direction, which was to only amend the Articles of Confederation. Instead they drafted a new Constitution. Yet, then as now, the delegates were only responsible to the charge given them by their states. Ten of the 12 colonies who sent delegates gave them freedom to draft a new Constitution, and 50 of the 52 signers acted consistent with their orders. For that reason no one back then considered the Convention as being a "runaway." That myth is a very recent revision of history.

Today, as then, each state, along with passing a Resolution calling for a Convention, also passes a bill that defines the authority of delegates sent to the Convention. States are limiting their delegates to the subject of the Resolution and replacing them at the convention if they go beyond their call. Some have gone further to mandate jail time. You need a majority of 26 states at the Convention to take any action. With 34 states limiting their delegates to the topic of their Resolution, there is no way to get the Convention to even consider another topic. Yet, even if there was, any radical amendment would still need to be approved by 38 states, and there is no reasonable fear that could happen. But there is a reasonable fear of economic collapse if we do nothing. And alternative plans that are pipe-dreams are akin to doing nothing. We cannot merely wait to elect enough fiscal conservatives with the courage to rein-in our debt. There is not enough time for that path to save us. Proponents of "Nullification" have no plan for how the States can stop Federal borrowing. States refusing to accept Federal Moneys will only see the Feds send that money to another state or find a new program within its "Enumerated Powers" to spend it on. And even if we could unravel the Federal Reserve and hand the keys for our Money Supply back to Congress, our Congress would still retain a virtually unlimited ability to continue to add to our debt.

Thomas Jefferson in his letter to John Taylor in 1798, said, "I wish it were possible to obtain a single amendment to our Constitution. I would be willing to depend on that alone for the reduction of the administration of our government; I mean an additional article taking from the Federal Government the power of borrowing."

Jefferson also said, in his letter to William Plumer in 1816, "I, however, place . . . public debt as the greatest of dangers to be feared. To preserve our Independence, we must not let our rulers load us with perpetual debt. If we run into such debts, we must be taxed in our meat and drink, in our necessities and in our comforts, in our labor and in our amusements. If we can prevent the government from wasting the labor of the people, under the pretense of caring for them, they will be happy."

The only way we can prevent the government from wasting the labor of the people is to limit their ability to spend. To do that, we must limit their ability to borrow. Forty-nine of the 50 States have BBAs. None are perfect. All have minor loopholes. But all are much, much better than nothing. Whatever the States propose won't be perfect. It will have loopholes and some will be necessary, like the ability to borrow during a declared war. But whatever the States propose, we can expect it will be much better than the virtually unlimited ability we've given the Feds to borrow and spend us into bankruptcy. The States must use Article V to propose a Federal BBA and save us from the economic destruction of our Republic. And, in addition to proposing a BBA, there is another vital action our States must lead to keep the Feds from reaching without permission into our back pockets. We have to reform our Tax System to end the layers of hidden taxes imbedded in the supply chain from taxing income at every level.

Think about how much more we pay for a loaf of bread because the Feds extract payroll tax from the farmer, the trucker who hauls the grain, the millworker who grinds the grain, another trucker, then the baker who makes the bread, then another trucker, then the stock clerk who puts the bread on the store shelf, then the checkout clerk who sells it to you. And the mountain of effort to collect income tax has spawned the massive growth of the IRS into a potent and dangerous political weapon for those in power. Yikes!

No wonder our Founding Fathers wrote the Constitution to limit the Feds to only collecting direct taxes from the states based on the census of the number of people in each state. We thought we knew better when we passed the 16th Amendment to begin taxing income. We were wrong.

We really can simplify our Tax Code and radically diminish the power of the IRS by passing The Fair Tax! It incorporates repealing the 16th Amendment and replacing the Income Tax with a consumption or sales tax. But it also provides every US citizen with a small, monthly check equal to the estimated tax on necessities. So effectively, no one pays any tax on basic food and shelter. And even though everyone pays the same percentage, the rich who buy more things end up paying the most in taxes.

It is simple, fair, and will radically transform our relationship with Government by ending Congress's ability to hide taxes and to micromanage our purchasing decisions. And it will eliminate, overnight, much of the lobbying that goes on now in Washington, fueled over the fight to win tax favors.

Plus, it will decimate the size and power of the IRS! Under the Fair Tax, the role of the IRS is reduced to tracking the collection of Sales Tax. There would be no more Income Tax Returns and thus no threat of audits or denials of tax-exempt status to wield as weapons against citizens. Your pastor won't have to worry about saying something too "political" from the pulpit! The fact that the monthly check to US citizens would not go to illegal aliens would force aliens to pay sales tax on necessities. That would reduce the magnet we have now drawing illegals across our borders!

As much sense as the Fair Tax makes and even though many Congressman profess to like it, we can't expect them to propose it. Ultimately, Congress gets too much power from the favors they can dish out in tax breaks under the current system. It is our States, which must lead this vital reform.

We need to engage our State Legislators and help them remember that it was not the Federal Government which formed our States. It was our States who formed the Federal Government. States are the parent and not the child and must rise up to assert themselves with their child that has grown unruly.

Wisconsin Patriots are invited to visit www.1776AmericanAction.com *to learn more and to sign petitions for the State-led BBA and Fair Tax Amendments.*

The *republican* Thomas Jefferson once declared "the

boisterous sea of liberty is never without a wave." Today timid Americans may prefer the calmness of the government sea for security at the expense of another man's liberty, but I prefer making waves fighting the Federal government tsunami rather than succumbing to its tyranny! Two hundred years ago the great statesman Daniel Webster declared: "Hold on, my friends, to the Constitution and to the Republic for which it stands. Miracles do not cluster and what happened once in 6,000 years may not happen again. Hold on to the Constitution."

In George Washington's April 30, 1789, Inaugural address, he not only spoke to his generation and those younger around him, he also spoke to you and me when he said:

"The preservation of the sacred fire of liberty, and the destiny of the *republican* model of government, are justly considered as deeply, perhaps as finally staked, on the experiment entrusted to the hands of the American people."

The freedom spirit of our Founders calls out to us today! Their freedom DNA is our freedom DNA; their love of life and liberty should be our love of life and liberty!

Our **Republic** beckons us to take action now to save it, to preserve this last and greatest bastion of freedom for our children and our children's children. Let us resolve to have the words that are inscribed across the top of the Liberty Bell from Leviticus 25:10 emblazoned in our hearts and declared from our lips; let us "proclaim liberty throughout all the land and unto all the inhabitants thereof!"

No, *Mother we cannot trust the Government,* but we can **Trust in God** to give us the strength and determination to put our hands to our Republic's falling flag and like those at Iwo Jima, raise it high for all the world to see that **this IS a sacred and sweet land of Liberty!**

Suggested Readings:

Lies the Government Told You: Myth, Power, and Deception in American History by Judge Andrew Napolitano

Fed Up! by Rick Perry

Liberty and Tyranny: A Conservative Manifesto by Mark R. Levin

Jake calling on Americans to but their hands on our Republic's falling Flag!

PART II

A SMALL SELECTION
OF JAKE JACOBS' IDEAS
ON GOVERNMENT

I.

OUR REPUBLIC UNDER GOD VERSUS THE GOD OF THE STATE

O ur Founding Fathers had a wonderful vision of a Republic under God where millions of citizens across this great land would shine the light of limited government, State sovereignty, the sanctity of all life and of marriage between one man and one woman. Our Founding Fathers' Judeo-Christian worldview proclaimed that man is more than matter in motion and "Marxist mud"; they believed that man is wonderfully made in the image of God.

Unlike the Radical Left of Europe and America today, our Founders did not worship the omnipotent STATE. Benito Mussolini, socialist turned fascist, loved to declare, "Tutto nello Stato, nulla contro lo Stato" (Everything in the State, nothing against the State). From time immemorial, mankind has desired to design an earthly kingdom without God where the State dictates humanity's destiny from crib to crypt. From Jean Jacque Rousseau's General Will, Robespierre's Reign of Terror, Lenin-Stalin's Soviet

Socialist rule of horror, Hitler's National Socialist ovens of hell, Castro's suppressive Cuban Communism, Mao's Marxist mass murder of millions and millions across Asia, to Saul Alinsky's Satan-dedicated book *Rule's for Radicals*, left-wing, atheistic "State-ism" has left in its diabolical and destructive dystopian path not only the eradication of freedom of religion, speech, press, and assembly, but the death of over one hundred million people in the twentieth century! *The Black Book of Communism: Crimes, Terror, Repression* is a book written by several European academics and edited by <u>Stéphane Courtois</u>.

Sadly, Statism-Socialism-Marxism is not dead. Its road to serfdom is alive and well around the world and in America. From the streets of Athens, Greece, and Paris, France, to New York City, and Madison, Wisconsin, and across America, Statism, Communism, Collectivism, and Big-government, elitist, central planning is raising its ugly, anti-American, totalitarian head attacking the traditional Judeo-Christian values that made this Republic under God the greatest form of government the world has ever seen. While sinful and not perfect, America is an otherwise exceptional place to live, and we have much to be proud of when we acknowledge Liberty's lifeblood: God Almighty.

The gods of the State from Julius Caesar to Joseph Stalin have always despised the God of Israel, the God of our Founding Fathers, the God in whom we trust. It was John Fitzgerald Kennedy who challenged the Statism of Soviet Socialism when he declared in his 1961 inaugural address: "The rights of man come not from the generosity of the State but from the hand of God." We must never forget and we must forever strive to educate our children, our friends, our neighbors, and anyone willing to listen that the origin of life and liberty is our Creator as described in our beautiful Declaration of Independence where God is also called in its sublime last paragraph "the Supreme Judge of the world."

It is not a coincidence that in the various socialist revolutions of France, Russia, China, Korea, Cuba, and Germany one of the first freedoms to disappear was freedom of religion, freedom of faith, as guillotines and gulags consumed millions of God's children. The gulag is not dead! Cultural and political gulags have taken over many of the key institutions in America as anti-Christian, politically correct, government schools, along with the ACLU, FFRF, the NEA, and thousands and thousands of Alinskyites, Progressives, and Socialists, disseminate atheistic Statism while denying our glorious Judeo-Christian foundation that is the key to freedom in any land.

When Samuel Adams, John Adams, and John Quincy Adams went to Harvard in the 1700s, they studied Hebrew, Greek, and Latin to learn from the great minds of antiquity from Aristotle and Cicero; from Moses and Jesus, and from Peter and Paul. In contrast, Barack Obama surrounded himself at Columbia and Harvard with neo-Marxist professors, structural feminists, and other radical socialists who taught him atheistic Marxist Critical Theory and Progressive anti-Constitutionalism that despises or denies our rich biblical heritage, republican form of limited government, and ultimately, the Sovereignty of YAHWEH-God and His people on earth.

II

SAM ADAMS – SO MUCH MORE THAN A BEER!

On college campuses today, young Americans' knowledge about one of America's great Founding Fathers is limited to "Sam Adams – a Boston Beer!" Additionally, America's youth sadly lack an understanding of the genius and greatness of our Founders and the wonderful Republic under God they created for us. Yes, "Sam Adams" is a Boston lager, but its namesake, Samuel Adams, was one of the primary movers and shakers for Liberty before, during and after the American Revolution. It was Sam's passion for freedom and his bravery to confront the most powerful Empire on the earth in 1770s that encouraged the Colonies to fight for independence from the tyrannical King of England and incompetent English Parliament. Thomas Jefferson wrote, "I asked myself, is this exactly in the spirit of the patriarch of liberty, Samuel Adams? He was the Father of the Revolution." John Adams confirms Jefferson's conviction when he declared, "Without the character of Samuel Adams, the true history of the American Revolution can never be written."

The key that unlocks Samuel Adams, and for that matter his cousins John Adams and John Quincy Adams and our Founders, was their love of **Law**. But not just any Law. The Adams family (no, not the creepy, spooky one), along with our Founding family loved **The Law of God**, the Law of our Creator who, according to the Declaration of Independence, is called the Supreme Judge of the world. As I watch the disdain and insane attitude President Obama has for the Rule of Law, our Constitutional Republic, and God's Law, I am convinced now more than ever that Americans must wake up and fight his BIG-government agenda, along with the progressive, socialist Democrats, and RINO (Republican in Name Only) Republicans who are destroying our Republic in leaps and bounds! In November 2014, we must elect men and women across America who actually believe and act in accordance to republican constitutional law and values that are anchored in God's eternal and gracious Law. Sam Adams' respect for the rule of law is reflected in his attitude to check his own emotional state of mind over the 1770 Boston Massacre by the British troops he despised quartering in Boston. While desiring to see the soldiers found guilty of murder, Sam did want them to have a fair trial and not death by a lawless Boston mob; therefore, he convinced his cousin John Adams, a Harvard-educated lawyer, to defend them. John Adams achieved their acquittal, and while Sam Adams believed they should have been executed for murder, he never wavered from his passion for due process and the rule of law. Founder of the Sons of Liberty and the Committee of Correspondence, Sam Adams wrote extensively on the necessity of the rule of Law based on its ultimate origin: God's Law. In his pamphlet *The Rights of the Colonists as Christians*, Adams writes,

"These may be best understood by reading and carefully studying the institutes of the great Law Giver and Head of the Christian Church, which are to be found clearly written and promulgated in the New Testament." During the signing of the Declaration of Independence in the summer of 1776, Samuel Adams declared, "We have this day restored the Sovereign to whom all men ought to be obedient. He reigns in heaven and from the rising to the setting of the sun let His kingdom come."

When drafting the Constitution of Massachusetts in 1779 with his cousin John Adams, Samuel exclaimed, "Among the objects of the Constitution of this Commonwealth, Liberty & Equality stand in a conspicuous light. It is the first article in our declaration of rights; all men are born free & equal, & have certain natural, essential & unalienable rights. In the supposed state of nature, all men are equally bound by the laws of nature, or to speak more properly, the laws of the Creator: They are imprinted by the finger of God on the heart of man."

In like manner John Adams wrote the following in his book, *A Defense of the Constitutions of Government of the United States of America*: "The moment the idea is admitted into society that property is not as sacred as the laws of

God, and that there is not a force of law and public justice
to protect it, anarchy and tyranny commence. If 'Thou shalt
not covet' and 'Thou shalt not steal' were not commandments of Heaven, they must be made inviolable precepts
in every society before it can be civilized or made free."

I quote Samuel and John Adams' reverence and utilization of God's Law extensively to give you a sense of the
importance they gave to it as the foundation of American
jurisprudence and our Constitutional republican form of
government. Unfortunately, in Post-Modern politically
correct America, our Judeo-Christian heritage entrenched
in these historical facts are no longer being taught in our
government schools or are being attacked and erased from
the records by the like of the ACLU and Freedom From
Religion Foundation.

John Quincy Adams, Sam Adams' cousin and the sixth
President of the United States, wrote this in his 1839 discourse, *The Jubilee of the Constitution:*

> "Fellow-citizens, the ark of your covenant is the
> Declaration of Independence. Your Mount Ebal,
> is the confederacy of separate state sovereignties,
> and your Mount Gerizim is the Constitution of
> the United States. In that scene of tremendous and
> awful solemnity, narrated in the Holy Scriptures,
> there is not a curse pronounced against the people
> upon Mount Ebal, not a blessing promised them
> upon Mount Gerizim, which your posterity may
> not suffer or enjoy, from your and their adher-
> ence to, or departure from, the principles of the

Declaration of Independence, practically interwo-
ven in the Constitution of the United States. Lay up
these principles, then, in your hearts, and in your
souls — bind them for signs upon your hands, that
they may be as frontlets between your eyes — teach
them to your children, speaking of them when sit-
ting in your houses, when walking by the way, when
lying down and when rising up — write them upon
the doorplates of your houses, and upon your gates
— cling to them as to the issues of life — adhere to
them as to the cords of your eternal salvation. So
may your children's children at the next return of
this day of jubilee, after a full century of experience
under your national Constitution, celebrate it again
in the full enjoyment of all the blessings recognized
by you in the commemoration of this day, and of
all the blessings promised to the children of Israel
upon Mount Gerizim, as the reward of obedience to
the law of God."

The Adamses and our Founders recognized that even
a republican philosophy of limited government in the
hands of sinful men separated from a relationship with our
Creator, the Supreme Judge of the world, and His Divine
Law would eventually deteriorate into despotism and the
arrogance of elitism. Our founders defined tyranny as:
"ruling apart from reference to and relationship with God
and His Law."

Where was it that the Samuel, John, and John Quincy
Adams learned this love and respect for the rule of law and

God's Law? They learned it at home from their Christian parents, in their churches, and at the then-Christian College of Harvard. Harvard was established in 1636 as America's first college to train men for the ministry and other vocations with the presupposition that education should be predicated upon the Scriptures as the starting point for wisdom and knowledge. Thus all graduates of Harvard had to know Hebrew, Greek, and Latin, as those languages allowed them the ability to more effectively understand the Old Testament, New Testament, and Classic Greek and Latin literature from Cicero and Plato to Augustine, Thomas Aquinas, and other great minds of Western civilization.

Harvard's original motto was *veritas christo et ecclesiae* or "Truth for Christ and the church." Harvard's original vision for its education is reflected in its "Rules and Precepts" for their students where it states:

> "Let every Student be plainly instructed, and earnestly pressed to consider well, the maine end of his life and studies is, to know God and Jesus Christ which is eternal life (John 17:3) and therefore to lay Christ in the bottome, as the only foundation of all sound knowledge and Learning. And seeing the Lord only giveth wisedome, Let every one seriously set himself by prayer in secret to seeke it of him (Prov. 2:3)."

Dr. Mark D. Roberts writes,

> Notice that *veritas christo et ecclesiae* does not

consist only of theological truth. This phrase
assumes that all truth is relevant to Christ and his
people, including the truth of physics, chemistry,
sociology, psychology, philosophy, and, well, you
name it. This view of truth denies the oft-made
distinction between the sacred and secular. It sees
all of creation, and therefore all of truth, as a result
of God and a reflection of God's own truthfulness.
Veritas christo et ecclesiae encourages people to
engage in all academic disciplines for the sake of
the kingdom of God.

That was the first motivation for the creation of the
Universities such as Oxford, Cambridge, Harvard and
Yale. The University was to be a place where one discovered
the wonder of the universe and the glory of the universe's
Creator, the God of the Bible, the God of Abraham, Isaac
and Jacob. The God of our Founders. This is why our
Founders' worldview was so steeped in a biblical worldview,
a scriptural worldview so prevalent that our presidents are
sworn in on the Bible, and the Bible's influence is seen pro-
fusely all over Washington, D.C., and across America in
the names of cities and counties, symbols, nomenclature,
proclamations, and legislation. The relationship between
God's Law and early American jurisprudence and legislation goes way back into the intellectual heart and mind of
Western civilization.

With the Christian evangelizing of Europe came the
dissemination of the Old and New Testaments, which were
full of laws, statues, adjudication, and jurisprudence. From

St. Patrick of Ireland to Alfred the Great of England all the way up to the influence of Dominican, Franciscan and Reformation scholastics, God's Law was an integral part of the development of a republican form of government. These republican ideas fused with God's Law are expressed throughout the writings of great philosophical minds such as Henry de Bracton, Edward Coke, Samuel Rutherford, John Locke, and one of the greatest legal minds of England, William Blackstone. Blackstone's 1765 *Commentaries on the Law of England* is so full of Scripture references it reads like a Bible commentary, and that commentary had a profound moral and legal influence on America's Founders. It is an undeniable historical FACT that God's Law as expressed in the Scriptures had not only a monumental impact on American Law and society, but was the inextricable life-blood and soul of our Republic under God!

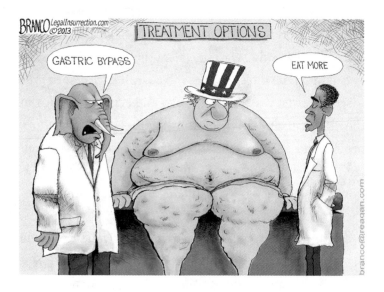

III.

TO TEA OR NOT TO TEA?
THAT IS THE QUESTION!

After Dave Brat's historic primary victory over one of the most powerful Republicans in Congress, both Democrats and Republicans and the Elite Media scrambled on how to spin this so-called Tea Party triumph. Ben Cunningham, president of the Nashville Tea Party, declared, "It has been an amazing shot in the arm. Dave Brat stated tea party principles simply, articulately, unapologetically, and he got elected doing that. It's just a great inspiration for everybody."

In contrast, Dave Brat doesn't like being tagged a Tea Partier. His dad, Paul Brat, says, "He doesn't like those labels," said Paul Brat, who's been watching his son shoot to the top of American political news with his stunning primary defeat Tuesday of House Majority Leader Eric Cantor. "He calls himself a Republican and runs on Republican principles."

What words or "labels" do we use when describing a political philosophy and governmental worldview? The political phenomenon labeled "The Tea Party" is hated by the Left and has been given the ugly label "Tea Baggers." It is maligned and ridiculed by some on the Right as loony and "the fringe." It is true that every political movement has its fringe and loony elements, but this populist citizen's movement is much more than that!

As a Constitutional *republican* (emphasis on the small *r*), I was intrigued by their movement when I heard them being attacked as "Brown shirts" or Nazis by Democrats and Progressives. On Tax Day, April 15, 2009, I went to watch their "Taxed Enough Already" rally in Appleton, Wisconsin. I didn't find Nazis, but I did observe over a thousand energized citizens expressing their concerns that the Federal government was taxing, spending, and expanding way too much. Known for my passion for Constitutional limited government, I was spotted in the crowd and asked to come up to speak. I did. I have been traveling America ever since then, speaking to thousands of American Patriots about the alarming explosion of the Federal government and the immediate need to rally the "Sons and Daughters of Liberty" against the Federal government's intrusion into our lives.

Throughout my travels, I have met many wonderful, hard-working Americans who are not "Baggers," "Nazis," or "Loony." On the contrary, I have experienced *a thinking citizens'* movement where they adore the Constitution as understood in its original context. They articulate the worldview of Federalists like James Madison and John Jay and republicans (Anti-Federalists) like Thomas Jefferson,

George Mason, and Patrick Henry. These citizens repudiate Big-government, Keynesian economics, are well-read in the Chicago School of Economics, and they are especially attuned to the Austrian School of Economics. They love F.A. Hayek's *Road to Serfdom*, Frederic Bastiat's *The Law*, Thomas Woods' *Who Killed the Constitution*, Ayn Rand's *Atlas Shrugged*, the works of Thomas Sowell, and sundry other lucid works on life and liberty.

They also understand the mind-set, worldview, and the Lefty Big-government advocates' devious mode of operation. They have read and understand the vile socialist philosophy of Barack Obama and Hillary Clinton's mentor – Saul Alinsky's *Rules for Radicals*. They are not fooled by the Elite Media's lies, biases, and distortion of the truth and reality of corruption in Washington, D.C.

We logically use labels all the time to communicate principles, philosophy, and ideas. Marx called his philosophy *Scientific Socialism*. Hitler labeled his *National Socialism*.

Our Founding Fathers used the label "democracy" as a derisive term describing a potential mob majority that would destroy life and liberty. Our Founders loved to use the term *republican* as an idea, a philosophy driven by the principles of a limited Federal government with few, very few enumerated powers, separation of powers, rule of law, trust in God, wise spending, reasonable taxes, and local control, while stressing popular and State sovereignty.

President Thomas Jefferson's 1801 inaugural address deals with those who attacked his love of the label "republican." He stated, "But every difference of opinion is not a difference of principle. We have called by different names brethren of the same principle. We are all *Republicans*, we are all Federalists ... I know, indeed, that some honest men fear that a *republican* government cannot be strong ... Let us, then, with courage and confidence pursue our own Federal and *Republican* principles ... and representative government." The *republican* Thomas Jefferson then goes on to encourage Americans to fight against the bulwark of "anti-*republican* tendencies" and to defend liberty with "the vital principle of *republics*."

Our Founders used labels to convey ideas and principles as we do today. **Liberty** in 1776 was defined in relationship to independency from government. Today Liberals have perverted that word to mean dependency on government, which ultimately leads to enslavement by government. The Tea Party movement understands that truth probably better than any political party in America today. That is why they are feared by Progressives and Liberals and dissed by the Republican establishment.

I prefer to call the Tea Party movement the **Liberty Party**, because they have gone far beyond the 1773 symbolism of dumping tea into the Boston Harbor. The Patriotic participants of this monumental movement come from all walks of American life, as they are the heart, mind, soul, and hands of authentic constitutional *republican* principles.

They are the personification of President Washington's 1789 inaugural words where he declared:

> "The preservation of that sacred fire of liberty and the destiny of the *Republican* model of

Government…are justly considered as deeply, perhaps as finally staked, on the experiment entrusted to the hands of the American people."

Let us extend our hands to those whose hands are in the battle and who understand that the sacredness of life and liberty in our land is in jeopardy. Let us join with them in raising our Republic's Flag high for the entire world to see: Liberty will not die on our watch!

IV.

OUR REPUBLIC VERSUS THE ELITE MEDIA'S WORLDVIEW

Okay, I will admit it: I watch MSNBC, CBS, ABC, NBC, and CNN.

I do so because my job as a teacher, writer, speaker, and citizen requires that I understand the worldview and mindset of the Elite Lefty Media that so profoundly feeds the minds of millions with lies and statistics that distort the reality of an egregious Federal government on steroids, destroying the Liberties of millions of Americans. Sometimes the inversion and perversion of the truth is propagated so badly and vociferously by the Elites that righteous indignation cries out of me in frustration, knowing that far too many Americans are being duped by the Goebbels-like lies.[3]

In the past few months, MSNBC has been running "Lean Forward" commercials with Chris Matthews and others

---

3   Reichskanzler Paul Joseph Goebbels was a German politician and Reich Minister of Propaganda in Nazi Germany from 1933 to 1945.

pontificating on the relationship between our Founders and BIG Progressive-Liberal Government. They bank on their viewers' ignorance and lack of historical knowledge of our Republic's founding so as to persuade them that the United States was created as something it wasn't and was never meant to be. Chris Matthews, during his thirty clips, opines on how Thomas Paine and Thomas Jefferson advocated "progressive" ideas about a "New World and a New Government" and having "it in our power to begin the world over." In these slick ads, you are left to believe that our Founders' worldview was Progressive and Liberal in the modern understanding of those terms that called for a large, bureaucratic, administrative State that circumvents the Constitution. Nothing could be further from the truth.

Historically, *liberal* or *liberty* in 1776 was defined in relationship to independency FROM government, not dependency on government or control by government. Today, Chris Matthews and the Elite Media's liberalism and progressivism is about more government, more dependency, more rules, more regulations, and more control BY government in our lives and in our land. The Elite Media and Matthews' worldview is in sharp contrast to the limited-government republicanism of our Founders in 1776 and 1787.

How did it happen that journalists and the Elite Media representatives have distorted historical context and implemented Orwellian language in their scripts and reporting?

I believe it's the textbooks being used!

The story is too long to tell here (you could read my

book *Mobocracy* for more historical details), but starting in the late 1880s, a slow "long, Marxist march" in our educational institutions took this nation on a trip with a hard turn to the Left that is driving out our Judeo-Christian heritage and distorting the republican limited-worldview of our Founding Fathers. This wonderful heritage is rarely, if ever, being taught in our government schools today as professors, educated in the 1960s and 1970s, have indoctrinated our K-12 and college-level teachers with Left Wing lies. A classic example of this is Todd Gitlin, one-time President of Students for a Democratic Society and professor from Columbia University, who declared: *"My generation of the New Left — a generation that grew as the [Vietnam] war went on — relinquished any title to patriotism without much sense of loss. All that was left to the Left was to unearth righteous traditions and cultivate them in universities. The much-mocked political correctness of the next academic generations was a consolation prize. We lost — we squandered the politics — but won the textbooks."*

Gitlin, being the cultural Marxist that he is, knew that education was the key to revolution from within. Those teachers and politically correct textbooks have shaped the cultural and political worldview and mindset of powerful people today like Barack Obama, Hillary Clinton, Harry Reid, Nancy Pelosi, many in Congress, and 90 percent of the Elite Media and academia. This is why the hard Lefty propagandist Chris Matthews is an admirer of Hillary Clinton and Barack Obama's favorite Marxist teacher

Saul Alinsky, who dedicated his book *Rules for Radicals* to Lucifer.

On Matthews' MSNBC program *Hardball*, he declared: "to reach back to one of our heroes from the past, from the Sixties, Saul Alinsky once said that even though both sides have flaws in their arguments and you can always find something nuanced about your own side you don't like and it's never perfect, you have to act in the end like there's simple black-and-white clarity between your side and the other side or you don't get anything done." Matthews concluded as he spoke on the topic of Obamacare with democratic socialist Senator Bernie Sanders, "I always try to remind myself of Saul Alinsky when I get confused."

To those of us who love our Republic under God and limited government, let us not get confused about the Elite Media's secular and BIG-government agenda! Chris Matthews and the Progressive-Liberal, BIG-government advocates are right about one thing: It is about "black and white." There is right and wrong in the universe. The universal, self-evident truth of our Founders' worldview is a profound belief and trust in the Creator of the universe, YAHWEH-God, the God of Abraham, Isaac and Jacob. He is the Sovereign source of Life and Liberty throughout the world, NOT Progressive-Liberal government. It is to that presupposition we must always be faithful.

V.

CONSERVATIVES AND CORRUPTION

Constitutional Conservatives like myself laughed with sadness when in 2006 Democratic Party leader Nancy Pelosi made the incredulous statement that, "We'll turn the most closed and corrupt Congress into the most open and honest Congress." We were not fooled to think that the corrupt Progressive Pelosi was actually going to change D.C. politics for the better.

Whether it's Democrats or Republicans in charge of Congress, Congress has lost its moral compass, as they have discovered that they can bribe the American people with the people's money. Yes, there are a few honest Democrats and Republicans in Congress, but far too many not only ignore the Law of the Land, our Constitution, but they are complicit with the President, the Supreme Court, and the American people in the destruction of the American Republic.

Did you say, "The American people, Jake?" Yes, I did – the American people.

The corruption of our Constitutional Republic is a two-way street. President James Garfield was spot-on in 1877 when he said: "Now more than ever before, the people are responsible for the character of their Congress. If that body be ignorant, reckless and corrupt, it is because the people tolerate ignorance, recklessness and corruption. If it be intelligent, brave and pure, it is because the people demand these high qualities to represent them in the national legislature ... If the next centennial does not find us a great nation ... it will be because those who represent the enterprise, the culture, and the morality of the nation do not aid in controlling the political forces."

The American people are not controlling the political forces with righteousness anymore. Many times when I speak at GOP, Conservative, Libertarian, and Tea Party events, I hear conservative citizens espouse limited constitutional government and rightly accuse the Federal government of spending too much money; and yet, at the same time they demand that the government not touch their Social Security, Medicare, and other entrenched entitlements they enjoy.

Yes, it is true there has been an ever-increasing destructive explosion of debt spending by the Federal Government and an ever-growing Federal encroachment on our Liberties, but much of our BIG-government problems stem from millions of Americans and many of them "contradictory conservatives" who demand that the Government leave their government goodies alone.

It is a sad commentary when States' Rights advocates passionately defend our wonderful Tenth Amendment and then freak out when the Federal government cuts their funding to State budgets. Far too many conservative governors, State legislatures, and municipal leaders feed at the Federal trough under the guise of funded and unfunded mandates, while knowing all along that the "Sugar Daddy Uncle Sam," unlike the States, has a Federal Reserve printing press and centralized collective power to disseminate funds across the land controlling more and more of our lives through National bureaucratic dictation.

Unfortunately, authentic and consistent Constitutional Conservatives are rare to find these days, and consequently, freedom in the American Republic dies.

When as a public school teacher I defended Wisconsin Governor Scott Walker, I knew I was going to lose some part of my government goodies such as a portion of my retirement and health care, but I was consistent within my Conservative philosophy by accepting Governor Walker's Conservative solution to our State's spending problem. Conservatives, are you willing to walk the walk when our Conservative representatives call for cuts and adjustments in Social Security, Medicare, and sundry other Federal programs?

When Governor Walker refused Obamacare's Medicaid expansion and adjusted Wisconsin's BadgerCare's eligibility, it was not only Liberals who cried bloody murder; many

Conservatives were just as agitated as they demanded that the government leave their entitlements alone.

My point is this: Progressives and Liberals in the last hundred years have not only succeeded in transforming our once-thriving Federal Republic into a BIG Brother National enterprise, they have also convinced, duped, and indoctrinated millions and millions of Americans into believing that a limited Federal government that functions solely within its enumerated constitutional parameters is antiquated, ineffectual, and heartless. Progressives, Liberals, Academics, Media, and our cultural icons have convinced Americans that "the government that governs best governs most" at both the Federal and State level.

Where are the courageous conservative voices declaring for "We the People" that "the government that governs best governs least?" Leave us alone, Uncle Sam! Leave us alone, State Governments! Yes, you too at times can act as egregious as the Federal Government!

Since 1913, the people have voted for or allowed the illegal creation of unconstitutional laws that we now must live with or pay for. From the Federal Reserve, Federal Income Tax, Social Security, Withholding Tax, direct election of Senators, FDR's Raw Deal, to LBJ's not-so-Great of a Society and thousands of other Federal laws, rules and regulations, the people are as much to blame as Washington, D.C.

The people, our fathers, mothers, grandfathers, and grandmothers, put the Progressives and Liberals in power, and now we reap what "We the People" have sown; now we must pay the Big-government piper and spender. We demand Federal government services and stuff and then scream about spending and taxes! Yes, the government lives beyond its means, but so do the people.

Millions of Americans have become indolent, indifferent, and insecure as they turn to government for comfort and security. Virtue is dying in America as we have forgotten the wisdom of our Founders – Founders like Benjamin Franklin who opined, "Only a virtuous people are capable of freedom. As nations become more corrupt and vicious, they have more need of masters."

Progressive masters and Liberals in government knew what they were doing when they distorted and twisted the original intent of our Founders' understanding of "general welfare" into Social Security, Medicare, a Great Society, Affordable Health Care, and myriads of other feel- good entitlement programs in D.C. They may all be unconstitutional, but the American sheep bleat to the government wolves, "forget the Constitution, feed me, comfort me, care for me, and give me security at my neighbors' expense!"

Our Federal Republic cannot endure when the public demands that their representatives confiscate the public's money or prints it to secure their stuff. Why do you think there are so few true-blue Conservatives that survive in Congress? Their survival rate is less than that of those on the bottom deck of the Titanic.

Do we Constitutional Conservatives have the guts to say, "We have met the enemy and he is us?" Let us first set in order our own house and then work to rebuild our nation's house.

By now you may be saying, "Jake, I thought you believed in a Constitutional Republic of limited government? In your speeches, articles, and books you disdain the explosion of unconstitutional Federal government corruption, spending, debt, and lies." I do! But how did it get to this point? We the people did it! We are the government and the government is us. We get what we deserve.

When Constitutional Conservative Senators and Congressmen fight for us in Washington D.C., do we not realize that they cannot undo over a hundred years of Progressive-Liberal unconstitutional corruption overnight? They are not only fighting anti-Constitutional forces by the National-Central government, they are fighting the demographic reality that millions and millions of Americans want to have their government cake and eat it too at our expense.

James Madison, the Father of our Constitution, stressed the importance of the character of the American people as the cornerstone of our Republic, when he said the following at the Virginia ratifying convention on June 20, 1788:

> "I go on this great republican principle, that the
> people will have virtue and intelligence to select
> men of virtue and wisdom. Is there no virtue
> among us? If there be not, we are in a wretched
> situation. No theoretical checks, no form of gov-
> ernment can render us secure. To suppose that
> any form of government will secure liberty or

happiness without any virtue in the people, is a chimerical idea. If there be sufficient virtue and intelligence in the community, it will be exercised in the selection of these men. So that we do not depend on their virtue, or put confidence in our rulers, but in the people who are to choose them."

In a similar spirit, the brilliant Roman Senator Cicero, who predicted the demise of the Roman Republic, said it best in 55 BC when he observed:

"The national budget must be balanced. The public debt must be reduced; the arrogance of the authorities must be moderated and controlled. Payments to foreign governments must be reduced. If the nation doesn't want to go bankrupt, people must again learn to work, instead of living on public assistance."

Our dying American Republic is being morphed from a Federal Republic into a Central-National Socialistic Democracy, where corruption rules from top to bottom and bottom to top. Let those of us who love our Republic start to make a difference at the bottom and elect and support those we put at the top.

THE FOUNDING FATHERS
AIN'T MY DADDY!

I used to teach an American Government class for a University of Wisconsin College. Last year my supervising Professor, in critiquing my class Syllabus, made this statement: "I prefer that you not refer to the Founders as Founding Fathers … my reason is that they aren't my daddy. My ancestors weren't even here at the time, and I think calling people your daddy is not as objective as political scientists should aim to be."

He was essentially asking me to ignore his subjectivity in a number of other areas in his teaching, such as his analysis of Wisconsin Governor Walker's Balanced Budget Act 10, which smacked more of a subjective, slanted, skewed, biased State employee than a so-called objective "political scientist," but I digress. Here's how I responded to his request:

> "I prefer to refer to the Founders as Founding
> Fathers. I'm in pretty good historical company
> here. From Daniel Webster's 1820 Discourse

Delivered at Plymouth to Abraham Lincoln's 1858
Electric Cord Speech, they and many other great
American Statesmen referred to our Founders
as Fathers and as ancestors all the time. They
and many others taught, as I do, that being an
American is ultimately not about ethnic or blood
identification; it is about one word – Freedom.
Therefore the self-evident reality that all men are
created equal and free makes us an 'American
Family related by Freedom.' Thus my freedom
ancestors, my freedom fathers, were here in 1776
and 1787, and as a free American citizen and a free
American teacher, I prefer to call them Fathers as it
conveys to my students the spirit of our Founders
and the blessings of Liberty."

I know it may sound strange, but I believe there is a
"Freedom DNA" that our ancestors and our Founding
Fathers inherited from God and passed on to Patriots who
love our Republic under God.

This politically correct Professor also stated, "I would also
prefer you not use the terminology 'American Constitutional
Republic under God' in your course description. As you
know from your research, there were all kinds of different
understandings of how religion related to politics at the
founding, and though most of the founders wanted God's
help, they also seemed to believe that they were setting up
a secular government."

I responded, "We will have to respectfully agree to disagree when it comes to our conclusions on the founding of

the United States in relationship to God and our Federal Government."

I took out the words *under God* in the Syllabus, although I did so under protest. The historian in me believes in historical context and IN CONTEXT our Founders never conceived of a Republic without God's guidance, wisdom, protection, and deliverance. Even the non-evangelical Christian Benjamin Franklin spoke of God and the need of prayer at the Constitutional Convention. The Father of the Constitution, James Madison, tells us that fact in his notes at the Constitutional Convention. Oops, did I call him "Father"?

The October 3, 1789, Thanksgiving Proclamation, passed by the House and the Senate and signed by President Washington, called for Prayer and Thanksgiving to God Almighty for our Constitution. In context that is not a secular expression about our Constitution; it is the framers of our Federal Constitution expressing a Republic under God. Here is a copy of that 1789 Thanksgiving Proclamation; notice as you read it the Christian-Biblical language used by the so- called secular Founders:

Thanksgiving Proclamation [New York, 3 October 1789]

By the President of the United States of America, a Proclamation.

Whereas it is the duty of all Nations to acknowledge the providence of Almighty God, to obey his will, to be grateful for his benefits, and humbly to implore his protection and favor – and whereas both Houses of Congress have by their joint Committee requested me to recommend to the People of the United States a day of public thanksgiving and prayer to be observed by acknowledging with grateful hearts the many signal favors of Almighty God especially by affording them an opportunity peaceably to establish a form of government for their safety and happiness.

Now therefore I do recommend and assign Thursday the 26th day of November next to be devoted by the People of these States to the service of that great and glorious Being, who is the beneficent Author of all the good that was, that is, or that will be – That we may then all unite in rendering unto him our sincere and humble thanks – for his kind care and protection of the People of this Country previous to their becoming a Nation – for the signal and manifold mercies, and the favorable interpositions of his Providence which we experienced in the course and conclusion of the late war – for the great degree of tranquility, union, and plenty, which we have since enjoyed – for the peaceable and rational manner, in which we have been enabled to establish constitutions of government for our safety and happiness, and particularly the national One now lately instituted – for the civil and religious liberty with which we are blessed; and the means we have of acquiring and diffusing useful knowledge; and in general for all the great and various favors which he hath been pleased to confer upon us.

and also that we may then unite in most humbly offering

*our prayers and supplications to the great Lord and Ruler
of Nations and beseech him to pardon our national and
other transgressions – to enable us all, whether in public
or private stations, to perform our several and relative
duties properly and punctually – to render our national
government a blessing to all the people, by constantly
being a Government of wise, just, and constitutional
laws, discreetly and faithfully executed and obeyed – to
protect and guide all Sovereigns and Nations (especially
such as have shewn kindness unto us) and to bless them
with good government, peace, and concord – To promote
the knowledge and practice of true religion and virtue,
and the encrease of science among them and us – and
generally to grant unto all Mankind such a degree of tem-
poral prosperity as he alone knows to be best.*

*Given under my hand at the City of New York the third
day of October in the year of our Lord 1789.*

Go: Washington

I know I said this earlier, but did you notice that this is
the FEDERAL republican government passing a Christian
Proclamation by both the House and the Senate and signed
by President George Washington? Politically Correct
Professors across America and the secular Left hate these
historical FACTS.

I continued to tell this Professor, "I do not want to
defend my Ph.D. Dissertation all over again, and you
probably don't want to hear it. But with all due respect,
a proper understanding of the separation of Church and

State does not mean that if our 'Founders seemed to believe they were setting up a secular government' that they did not invoke His name, and publicly trust in Him within a legal Constitutional framework. *They did so all the time.* There is too much historical evidence contrary to that. The world's largest library, the Library of Congress, confirms what I'm saying and confirms our Federal Republic's relationship to God."

(Readers, please copy and paste this link; it is FULL of historical gems to sharpen your Founding Fathers' worldview: http://www.loc.gov/exhibits/religion/rel06.html)

I went on to say, "To state in my syllabus and teachings 'under God' is not only in the tradition of Federal Law of 1956, but reflects the historical context at the time of the Constitution's creation and after its establishment. They used such 'God' language all the time." I could give a thousand examples, but the following links explain the historical context I cannot ignore: (Readers, once again check this stuff out!)

http://founders.archives.gov/documents/
Washington/05-04-02-0091/

Here is the original from the National Archives.

http://www.archives.gov/historical-docs/
todays-doc/?dod-date=1123

The cultural and political war to destroy our Republic under God intensifies and expands in America in our educational institutions and has been taken over by secular, Progressive-Liberal academicians who do not want us to teach the Christian truth to our youth and that the Founding Fathers, while not perfect, were a gift sent to us by God Almighty.

Since this reprimand last year by my supervising Professor, I have not been asked to teach this American Government class anymore; in other words, I was fired.

So be it.

I will not be silent on these most essential issues that must be taught to young Americans. We need our youth to recapture the beauty of our Republic under God as given to us by our ancestors and our Founding Fathers, so they can carry the mantle of Freedom and Liberty into the future. Liberty always comes at a cost!

TRUST BUT VERIFY

My son Joseph works for Apple and is one of their "Geniuses." Yes, he makes his Baby Boomer Dad feel pretty dumb when I ask questions about Social Media and how to work my MacBookPro. I utilize Facebook, Twitter, Linkedin, etc., and run my website **jjusa.org**. As many of you know, the "information highway" in cyberspace is full of a zillion sources of ideas, opinions, philosophies, propaganda, good information, and much bad disinformation. Like you, at times I can be inundated with "information" that claims to have the latest titillating scandalous scoop on our political opponents. Conservative Readers Beware!

My fellow Constitutional Conservatives, I ask you this question with all sincerity:

How are Americans to discern where the "truth" is in today's plethora of information sources, from blog articles, media outlets, think tanks, advocacy groups, etc.? Much, if not most, of what is out there is rubbish!

In my classroom, I always stress "learning to discern"

"trusting but verifying," and "not rushing to judgment" without first doing a thorough investigation of the alleged facts. It is easy to jump on the latest "fact" bandwagon, declaring they heard Barack Obama say this or that, or that Nancy Pelosi said that, only to find out later "Conservatives" were telling lies about them. You should see some of the unprofessional and poorly researched fabrication that is sent to me by well-meaning Patriots who failed to verify the garbage sent to them before they forward it across America.

The latest one sent to me was the Conservative claim that Senator Barack Obama appeared on *Meet the Press*, September 7, 2008, claiming he wanted to replace the Stars and Stripes with a new flag and our national anthem with the song "I'd Like to Teach the World to Sing." That silly claim itself should have been a "Red Flag alert" to verify the alleged *Meet the Press* statement by Obama. FACT: This claim or charge against Obama never happened! We have enough corruption, deception, and lies going on in Washington, D.C., by Obama and the Left without having to contend with Conservatives' fabrications, lies, and deception.

There are many silly and many very sophisticated claims and charges out there that are accepted hook, line, and sinker by good Conservatives who should know better and must be more disciplined to know better. It is human nature to apply the "Fonz Syndrome" when we are confronted with information or facts that prove us to be in error. If we are intellectually honest, we should be willing to admit we were "wrooo-nnng" and then move on to defend the Conservative cause with as much accuracy and truth as humanly possible. On occasion when I too have been guilty of rushing to judgment or drawing poor conclusions, I have had to simply admit that I was wrong. It is okay to readjust your thinking if facts determine a more truthful and wise way to accomplish your ultimate goal. Truth must be our ultimate goal.

We must all strive to be as accurate and truthful as possible when we as Conservatives confront and battle Big-government advocates in Washington, D.C. When a Conservative group distorts, perverts, or exaggerates an issue, I am just as upset, if not more so, than when a Progressive-Liberal group does. We should know better. We must have a standard of truth and integrity above the Left; otherwise, we will never win our righteous Constitutional Conservative cause.

Some Conservative and Tea Party organizations dear to my heart have on occasion rushed to judgment or distorted information to persuade Americans on an issue or bring money into their coffers. This is what the Left is all too often guilty of and should not be the mode of operation for the Right's righteous cause. Knowing the truth with clarity and accuracy is not easy. It requires study, research, discipline, discernment, and investigation. In our hurried world today, too many of us rely on sound bites, talking points, or an Internet article or two to shape our conclusions on very serious issues.

This does not nullify our Constitutional Conservative cause. However, honesty not only clarifies our cause, it solidifies the integrity of our arguments before man and God. We must strive for truth, not "party" or "group" loyalty done with stupidity. As a historian, I have trained myself with this Golden Rule, and I want to encourage my fellow American Conservatives to apply this rule in your research and articulation of Constitutional republican values. If you do, then when you discuss and debate the issues, you will have the confidence of truth within you and beside you, fighting as a righteous Warrior for Liberty!

NO LABELS

Warning! You might not like my "labeling ways" in this article on the No Label Group in Washington, D.C., which has three Wisconsin Congressmen's involvement: Sean Duffy, Tom Petri and Reid Ribble. I know all three and respect them VERY much, BUT the Constitutional Conservative republican in me is concerned. As I constructed this article in my mind while working out at the gym, I knew I would step on toes and toes close to home. A dear friend of mine, Congressman Reid Ribble from Wisconsin's 8th District, recently has been discussing his involvement with *No Labels*, a Congressional group of eighty-one members to date. I have told Reid before that it is easy for me to speak and write on my concerns about corruption in Washington, D.C., but very difficult to actually change that corruption. This article is not meant as a pot shot. If I am too vociferous and ungracious here, please forgive me, but my heart calls me to write this critique of *No Labels*. And before I continue with my article on words, labels, and political identification, let me say that I have the utmost respect, admiration, and love for Reid Ribble, as he is the real deal, a Christian Conservative (oops, sorry for the label) who loves God, his family, and America like few men I know. I've known Reid since our high school years at Appleton High School East. We were called "The Patriots," and Reid is a true Patriot. So my issue here is not so much with Reid's association and advocacy of the *No Labels* group in Congress, but with *No Label's* fuzzy thinking on words and labels and wishful thinking that believes if we can get along without labeling each other, our problems will go away.

As earlier stated, I write this article with trepidation that I might offend my friends and fellow compatriots, but with the realization that our Federal government is in serious dysfunction and because America's central government has the nefarious nature of beating its own into compliance, I am compelled to write.

In my various conversations with Senators and Congressmen over the last few years, they tell me that they truly have very LITTLE power and that the Congressional Oligarchs and D.C. bureaucrats call most of the shots as they pass discombobulated and convoluted bills without reading so they would know what was in them or to maintain their pork barreling power.

Thus, I'm more convinced than ever that the KEY to saving America is as our Founders stated: at the local and State level, NOT the Federal level.

We MUST find a way to nullify the evil ACTS of a corrupt Federal government gone amuck and determined to destroy our Freedoms. *No Labels* from my perspective is a waste of time. Like most liberal rhetoric, it sounds good on paper and makes sweet sound bites, but like castrated sheep, *No Labels* does next to nothing to STOP the Federal government wolves at our door. Here is my thinking:

I call and label myself a Constitutional Conservative republican.

For good reason. Labels convey ideas. Some ideas put into action secure Liberty while other ideas put into action destroy Freedom. I label myself this way unabashedly and proudly because I believe the U.S. Constitution to be one of THE most amazing government documents in World History, and it is the Law of the Land. I call myself a republican small "r" because many of our Founders such as Washington, Jefferson, and Madison proudly labeled themselves republicans. The Founders labeled the United States a Constitutional republic, not a democracy.

I label myself a Conservative because modern Conservatives actually express ancient classic liberalism's belief in a limited Federal government, local control, individual freedom, traditional values that make for a healthy and holy society, and a number of checks and balances to STOP the government's natural desire to grow and destroy the Life and Liberty of "We the People."

If you go to *No Labels'* website under *Who We ARE* they state: "*No Labels* is a movement of Democrats, Republicans and everyone in between dedicated to promoting a new politics of problem solving. While many powerful interest groups in Washington wield influence that effectively pulls leaders and the political parties apart, *No Labels'* mission is different – it's about fixing, not fighting."

There you have it. *No Labels* is about "fixing, not fighting." *No Labels* even sells *No Labels* products, such as coffee cups, BBQ aprons, water bottles, baby rib t-shirts, and even a hat "labeled" (pun intended) "The kissing hat," where the Democrat donkey is kissing the Republican elephant.

Kissing each other with no fighting, no labeling, and an oft-repeated mantra "Not Left, not Right, forward." This is an admirable goal to fix the nation's problems without fighting. Their intention to move America forward is a wonderful platitude, but will it work in the real world of fallen, corrupt, and sinful man?

Here's where I must depart from *No Labels'* declarative "can't we all get along?" No we can't! And here's why: Human Nature and Truth.

On Truth: Our Declaration of Independence declares, "We hold these truths to be self- evident." Our Founders always presupposed in their argumentation and advocacy for Freedom and Liberty from tyrannical government that Truth was essential for its success. When they argued and, yes, dare I say fought their case, they did so with ideas from the Scriptures and great thinkers from Western civilization. Our Founders argued their case with the conviction that there were good ideas and bad ideas, that there was right and wrong, and that there were Freedom fighters and Freedom destroyers. They did so with the conviction that declared, "Give me Liberty or Give me Death!" and as the despotic British Government executed them, they cried out, "I only regret that I have but one life to lose for my country!"

While Truth calls us to respect each other's humanity, Truth also calls us to call out deniers of Truth and destroyers of Life and Liberty. Such destroyers are in Congress, and some are in the *No Labels 81* who call and label themselves Progressives and Liberals.

By the way, many so-called Conservatives in Congress today are deniers of Truth.

On Human Nature: In Federalist Paper Number 51, James Madison states: "If men were angels, no government would be necessary. If angels were to govern men, neither external nor internal controls on government would be necessary. In framing a government which is to be administered by men over men, the great difficulty lies in this: you must first enable the government to control the governed; and in the next place oblige it to control itself. A dependence on the people is, no doubt, the primary control on the government; but experience has taught mankind the necessity of auxiliary precautions."

Here is where *No Labels* misses the mark with their good intentions and peaceful platitudes. They fail to grasp the reality of human nature and the bloody, dirty, and raucous nature of securing freedom. From time immemorial, most of humanity and politicians have not been angels, and governments have not been angelic; thus, we fought a War to secure Liberty. Thus, we fought a Civil War to destroy slavery. Thus, we fought myriads of civil rights battles to end segregation and discrimination. American history is replete with bold argumentation and battling for truth over the lies of corrupt men, politicians, and government at the local, state, and federal levels.

Did not the Prince of Peace call corrupt leaders in his day "brood of vipers and white washed tombs?" Did He not speak of hell more than heaven and that two swords were enough?

I do not for a moment doubt the decent and good intentions of many "No Labelers." Their spirit and hearts' desire is to respectfully and peacefully fix and solve our problems. However, with all due respect, their intentions are not a path forward to heavenly solutions but the continued Federal government's *Road to Serfdom*, a road that is a muddled moderate complacency that perpetuates government inefficacy and the continued expansion of the Federal government's control over the sovereign people! It is unrealistic, grandiose, and naive wishful thinking that does not have the ability to STOP the ugly explosion of our Federal government. Yes, they have nibbled at the edges of the general government's BIG Brother expansion, but to quote William Wallace in the movie *Braveheart*:

> "You're so concerned with squabbling for the scraps from Longshank's table that you've missed your God-given right to something better. There is a difference between us. You think the people of this country exist to provide you with position. I think your position exists to provide those people with freedom. And I go to make sure that they have it."

No Labels is so concerned with squabbling for the scraps from Obama's and Uncle Sam's table that they've missed their God-given duty to DO something better! While well-intended and good-hearted Republicans who call themselves Conservatives are joining arm and arm with "Progressives, Liberals and everyone in between," they are failing to recognize that their position in Washington, D.C., exists to provide "we the people" with freedom and not an ineffectual public relations stunt that only scratches the surface of corrupt D.C. politics. America needs BOLD and BIG action NOW! Not smoke and mirrors.

At the end of *No Labels' Who We Are*, they state with touchy-feely, all-inclusive, do good-ism rhetoric:

> "*No Labels* does not expect anyone to shed his or her political identity when they join our movement. We are a 'come-as-you-are' community of passionate liberals, progressives, moderates, conservatives and everyone on the political spectrum. It's precisely our diversity that defines our group and makes us stronger. We are united by the conviction that people of all different beliefs can set aside the labels and together start solving America's problems."

A "community of proud liberals, progressives, moderates, conservatives and everyone on the political spectrum – it's precisely our diversity – that makes us stronger?" This convoluted thinking defies the law of non-contradiction "where two antithetical ideas cannot both be true at the same time and in the same sense, X cannot be non-X. A truthful idea cannot 'be' and 'not be' simultaneously. And nothing that is true can be self-contradictory or inconsistent with any other truth. All logic depends on this simple principle. Rational thought and meaningful discourse demand it. To deny it is to deny all truth in one fell swoop."

The ideas of "passionate" Progressivism-Liberalism and Conservatism cannot peacefully co-exist as a "movement," "group," or "community"; they are the antithesis of each other. They are bi-polar opposites. Progressivism-Liberalism is regressive, wrong, and destructive to Liberty, while Conservatism, when followed and practiced by those brave enough to declare it, is the vanguard that advances and preserves Freedom in America! Throughout the ages, philosophers, theologians, and thinkers have used labels for a simple reason – Communication.

Words and labels have meaning and ideas have consequences. Our Founders were profound students of languages, words, and ideas. They could read Aristotle in Greek, Cicero in Latin, and Moses in Hebrew. They copied words and crafted words carefully to convey ideas precisely. They used words and ideas that were antagonistic and words and ideas that were protagonist. They labeled words and ideas all the time: Tories and Whigs, Federalists and Anti-Federalists, Liberty versus Tyranny, Freedom versus Despotism. A classic example of their word use and labeling was democracy versus republicanism.

If you look at the history of progressivism and modern liberalism, they love using the word democracy for our form of government because they despise our Constitutional Republic. On the other hand, Conservatives, being true to our Founders and our Constitution's Article 4 section 4, love using the word republic or republicanism. In 1776 or 1787 no respectable person called or labeled him or herself a democrat. Why? Because democracy was equated with tyranny, while republicanism was equated with liberty. That is why Thomas Jefferson and many of our Founders proudly labeled themselves republicans, as the word conveyed a political philosophy of limited government with enumerated powers, local control, and sovereignty of the people over the State and State sovereignty over the potential corruption of the general-Federal government. *No Labels* ignores the corrosion of Freedom in America and the explosion of the Federal government and wants the rest of us to join with the groups that label and call themselves Progressives (ask Hillary Clinton what she labels or calls herself; you'll be hearing that word a lot when she runs for President in 2015-2016), or Liberals that have for the last hundred years denigrated, obfuscated, and ignored our Constitution. The Sovereign people of America are in a cultural and political war initiated by the Left, driven by Liberals, perpetuated by Progressives, and downplayed by establishment Republicans who knowingly or unknowingly, with so-called good intentions are destroying individual Liberty and transforming our Republic under God into democratic-socialism under the State.

Liberals and others have told us that to use the label *War* is inappropriate in today's political world. Obviously, by now you know I profoundly disagree. To everything there is a season, a time for peace and a time for war. Our Founding Fathers stopped a tyrannical King through war, our Fathers defeated National Socialism and Soviet Socialism through war. South Korea and Western Europe are free because we fought a Cold War. Today's war is an enemy within – within our halls of Congress, within our Courts, within the White House, within the Culture, within Academia, Hollywood, and the Media.

I for one cannot stand idly by while *No Labels* gentlemen and gentle-ladies cry, peace, peace – but there is no peace. The War has actually begun! Our fellow compatriots are already in the battlefields across America; they are working at the local level in villages, town halls, cities, counties, and State Capitols daring to corrupt Washington, D.C.; "is life so dear; or peace so sweet, as to be purchased at the price of chains and slavery? Forbid it, Almighty God!"

Our glorious Stars and Stripes is falling. Our Republic is calling out to us to preserve the sacred fire of liberty with our hands and hearts in action, raising Old Glory to the greatness she once knew. Constitutional Conservative republican Representatives in Washington, D.C. – don't waste our valuable time! Say NO to *No Labels* and YES to BOLD Constitutional Action now! Fight for the Sovereign People!

ABOUT THE AUTHOR

Dr. Jake Jacobs has been married for twenty-nine years to his lovely wife Lori and has two children, Joseph, 25, and Anastasia, 22. When he's not writing, teaching or speaking, he loves watching the Green Bay Packers and enjoys his fire pit at night, watching the Heavens declare God's Glory.

He is president and founder of the Politically Incorrect Institute and has degrees in American History and Biblical and Judeo-Christian Studies from Arizona State University, Arizona College of the Bible, Ashland Theological Seminary, and North-West University. Dr. Jacobs has spent more than twenty-seven years at the public and private high school system and at the college level, teaching his passion for our Constitutional Republic under God, all the while stressing historical correctness in the face of politically correct intimidation by the academic establishment.

Dr. Jacobs has publicly defended Wisconsin Governor Scott Walker on *Fox & Friends* and is a regular guest at Young American Foundation's Reagan Ranch Center, Conservative Conferences, CPACs, College Campuses,

Republican and Tea Party events, and at various civic and church events. He is a dynamic and energized speaker, writer, and historian who will not only get your audience's attention, but also move them to action!

To schedule Dr. Jacobs for your event, contact him at www.jjusa.org.

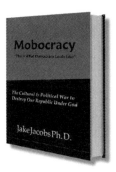

Wake up America, before it is too late, before we have communism in America! The mobocrats mean business. Watch the culture war, study the mob, listen to their words and watch their ways and understand their demands to change and transform our Republic under God. The original tea party movement, our Founders, warned us that if we were to keep our Republic we would always have to remain diligent to the cause of freedom and vigilantly aware of those who would under the guise of freedom destroy life and liberty.

America is under attack. Its constitutional rights, institutions and values are under daily assault. But the principal culprits are not foreign terrorists. They are influential and powerful Americans, applying Marxist theory, secretly stirring up disunion and disloyalty in the shifting shadows of the Democratic Party. Read this book. Pray for our country. Teach your children the Biblical principles our founders believed and lived. And support the men and women who are willing to set everything else aside and speak up for the truth. Semper Fi to the Republic!

Available from Amazon, and anywhere books are sold

If you enjoyed this book, you may also enjoy other titles by the same publisher

Use coupon code **"25"** to **save 25%**
when shopping at
www.lifesentencepublishing.com

'Eradicate' identifies two major problems causing the spiritual and moral decline in our country: the secular agenda to blot out God, and the apathy of Christians. This book will expose the anti-Christian movements in America and give you a thorough understanding of the foundational battle for truth. With 78% of Americans claiming to be Christians, how did it get to the point where Christianity is having less of an influence on our culture than culture is having on Christianity? Too many believers have conformed to our culture and we're now suffering the consequences as a nation.

Enemy forces continue to destroy this nation by attacking America's Judeo-Christian roots from within. This book will investigate government, media, Hollywood, public schools, our culture of death, and the push toward socialism and Marxism. You'll see how some churches and leaders are diluting the Word of God weakening the witness of believers. You may be outraged as this book exposes how sin is being openly promoted, yet encouraged because God is still in control. There's a remnant of committed Christians resisting evil and standing in the way. The choice is ours: who or what will we give our allegiance to, God or man; to Jesus Christ or to culture and politics? As Christians, our loyalties must not be divided any longer or America may be lost.

About the Author

David Fiorazo is an author, radio personality, actor, blogger, and speaker. He has over 30 years of experience in the broadcasting and entertainment industries. David recommitted his life to Jesus Christ in 1987 and as he traveled across America, he witnessed the moral decay and spiritual decline of our Republic under God that continues today.